Contents

D1506256

COMING OUT EVERY DAY

By Bret K. Johnson, Ph.D.

New Harbinger Publications

Publisher's Note

This publication is designed to provide accurate and authoritative information in regard to the subject matter covered. It is sold with the understanding that the publisher is not engaged in rendering psychological, financial, legal, or other professional services. If expert assistance or counseling is needed, the services of a competent professional should be sought.

Copyright © 1997 Bret K. Johnson, Ph.D.
New Harbinger Publications, Inc.
5674 Shattuck Avenue
Oakland, CA 94609

Cover design by Ice King Design.
Text design by Tracy Marie Powell.

Distributed in the U.S.A. by Publishers Group West; in Canada by Raincoast Books; in Great Britain by Airlift Book Company, Ltd.; in South Africa by Real Books, Ltd.; in Australia by Boobook; and in New Zealand by Tandem Press.

New Harbinger Publications website address: www.newharbinger.com

Library of Congress Catalog Number: 96-71153

ISBN 1-57224-064-4 paperback

Printed in the United States of America using recycled paper.

10 9 8 7 6 5 4 3 2

From the first day I uttered, "I'm Gay," there have been those who have stood by me through tough, confusing times. I'm truly grateful for the love, patience, and respect. My friends, family, and colleagues have supported and inspired me to create this for all GBQ men who struggle with their innermost desires and fears.

To my dear friends Tara Crowley, Lynne Christiansen, Greg Bruno, and Patrick Meyer, thank you for your undying support, love, acceptance, and a place to crash.

Specific thanks to my friends/mentors/colleagues Pam Kangas and Jerry Solomon for the years of laughter and enlightenment and honest feedback and encouragement.

Thanks to Alan Fletcher and Deb Abbott of JFKU for their warm wishes, and unfettered and scholarly ideas.

Gratitude to my personal editor, Carol Henry who shaped and shined this book from its early origins.

Farrin Jacobs and Kristin Beck at New Harbinger have truly made rewrites and the entire process engaging, personally satisfying, and painless. And thanks to Gayle Zanca for her editorial expertise.

To Roger Mills and Cathy Casey for their comments and guidance about POM.

Special appreciation to Ellen Bass and Kate Kaufman for the care, time, and help of their studied eyes. And to Laura Davis for her experience and early inspiration.

To my friends over the years, for their love and support I am eternally grateful: Larry Martin, Gary Hayes, Denise Verollini, Linda Thorsen, Win Schacter, and Jon Anderson.

I will always appreciate Gary Maddocks for, among other things, helping me to really look at myself. His memory lives on in the spirit of this book.

To my parents, Barbara and Jerry Cheney, Pete and Nell Johnson, and my sisters, Stacey and Stephanie, for their understanding, willingness to grow and accept, and ultimate respect and faith in me.

I am forever grateful to my partner, Paul, for his continued love, humor, his ability to teach me about loyalty and generosity, his commitment to our relationship, and for seeing this book through from start to finish—all those hours reading the manuscript, listening to my stories, and devoting time to this project.

Lastly, to all the men from youth to adulthood who have continued to surprise and inspire me with their own unique journeys; they are the inspiration for the stories, anecdotes, and exercises in this book. Thank you for your courage and passion. Hopefully, your messages will serve to mentor all the GBQ readers who undertake the labor of love of coming out every day.

Introduction

The Lifelong Process of Coming Out

Better than I've ever felt in my life.

—Rep. Gerry Studds (D-Mass), when
asked how he felt after coming out

Coming out has been described by many gay and bisexual men as "up-lifting," "a removal of burdens and freeing of spirits," "the release of mental and emotional energy to pursue life, liberty, and happiness." You may have already discovered, however, that coming out doesn't end when you tell your family and friends. It is a continuing process that deepens your identity, enriches your relationships, and nourishes your soul.

For a long time, gay, bisexual, and questioning (GBQ) men have likened coming out to emerging from a closet of secrets. (We'll talk more about the GBQ acronym later.) This closet holds a lot: special, tender feelings; wild and spontaneous erotic desires; shame and fear of stigmatization and discrimination; and the conflicts of being different from the majority. Your closet may have kept you distanced or even isolated from people you love; it may also have helped you maintain a safe distance from those you mistrust. It's likely that your closet has been a mixed blessing in a heterosexual world you've not yet found your place in.

Every GBQ man comes out in his own unique way. Some guys burst out of the closet with all the vigor of an Olympic track star after the starting gun. Some take cautious steps at first, and others have several starts and stops before crossing the finish line. But is there really a finish line?

Whether you're coming out to others or to yourself, coming to terms with your sexuality is a lifetime process. It doesn't stop when you've told your mother, child, or roommate. However, coming out certainly becomes less burdensome after the first step, and decisions gradually become easier to make about whom to tell and when. In fact, some people claim you get to the point where you never think about your sexual orientation at all—it's just who you are and others can take you or leave you. Coming out inside—acknowledging and honoring the shadows and the light of your GBQ soul—is a parallel process to coming out to others. Coming out both internally and externally is what makes your sexual orientation a natural part of your whole being.

Statistics, Generalizations, and Opinions

Although *Coming Out Every Day* includes facts and statistics gathered through research, I believe scientific re- search on GBQ issues still has a long way to go. Caution is therefore in order in inter- preting the research. I'll comment more on the limitations of research later in this chapter. For the dis- cussions in this book, I have drawn heavily from my own and others' *clinical experience*.

Much of your coming-out process occurs every day without any help from a book. It happens in the course of the normal emotional growth you experience as you interact with the people you care about and work with, and even some of the people who are peripheral to your life. In the process of reading this book, you may decide you want to come out to the grocery clerk, your neighbor, or your mortgage lender—and that's okay. More likely, however, you're seeking to be more comfortable with being gay or bisexual, or you're looking for help in coming out for the first time to loved ones. Whatever your situation, through reading this book and living life, you will find ways to accept your sexual orientation as an integral part of who you are.

How This Book Can Help

You may be reading this book to better understand your identity as a GBQ man, to improve your relationships, or to find guidance for how to go about coming out. Maybe you want to work on your self-esteem, or fine-tune your emotional or spiritual well-being. All of these goals are relevant to the exploration you're undertaking with this book.

You may be relieved to know that you are not alone or crazy. Throughout these pages, you'll encounter the experiences of men in circumstances similar to your own going through various stages of the coming-out process. Working through the exercises in this book, at your own pace, will improve your self-understanding. You'll be encouraged to think through the range of emotions that accompany being a GBQ man. You'll discover what you want to accomplish and how to act on these discoveries in several essential areas of GBQ life. These areas include

- Exploring your identity as it has changed through your life cycle

- Recognizing and changing personality and behavioral obstacles

- Finding and improving supportive relationships

- Ascertaining the how-tos and who-tos of coming out as a GBQ man

- Identifying your needs in sex and intimacy

- Getting healthier—spiritually, emotionally, and physically

- Gaining confidence and pride in being GBQ

- Exploring strategies to overcome prejudice and discrimination

Coming Out Every Day will not only put you in touch with your innate wisdom, but it will help you become proactive in your GBQ life journey. Reading this book will guide you to strengthen yourself in some new ways.

Using This Book to Meet Your Needs

Coming Out Every Day was written to be read sequentially from beginning to end. The text of the chapters, as well as the exercises, build on one another. As a group, they will enhance your personal learning, growth, and healing.

That said, ultimately this is your book to use as you see fit. Whether it sits on your nightstand for occasional contemplation or is devoured in a single sitting on a dark and windy night, you should read it when you want to read it, and do only the exercises you want to do. Write notes in the margins if you feel like it. Use it as a personal journal of your coming-out process. Use it to mark your own development and set goals for yourself. Go back over sections you want to explore in more depth, reread your writings, and compare them to present feelings. Share it. Use it as a jumping-off point for psychotherapy. Take it to therapy sessions when you discuss important experiences.

Before reading any further, let's look at what you think you want from this book. Check as many items as you want in the following list. (It will probably be interesting to you later, after you've finished the book, to see how many of your goals you attained, and how many you hadn't even considered!)

I want to use this book

_____ As a general personal-growth tool

_____ As a guide to coming out to myself

_____ As a guide to help me come out to others

_____ To help me decide when I want to come out, to whom, and how I want to do it

_____ For help with knowing how to express my sexuality

_____ To define my sexual orientation

_____ To find out about the "developmental life cycle" and where I am in this cycle

_____ To learn strategies for managing the feelings I have about coming out

_____ As a journal and record of my coming-out experiences

_____ To help stop destructive patterns in my behavior

_____ To help me understand why I feel ashamed and guilty

_____ To increase my confidence as a gay, bisexual, or questioning man

_____ To better understand my sexuality

_____ To learn how to "be myself" as a gay or bisexual man

_____ To learn ways of resisting society's stereotyping of being gay or bisexual

_____ To help me analyze and face painful feelings

_____ To find out about ways to be safe sexually

_____ As guidance in finding and building supportive relationships

_____ For help in building more intimate relationships

_____ For help in developing healthier relationships of all kinds

_____ As a guide to improving my relationship with my family

_____ For ways to improve my overall emotional health

_____ To find out about improving my physical (and sexual) health

_____ For help in acknowledging and developing my spiritual side

_____ To gain understanding of homophobia and prejudice

_____ To help me worry less about what others think of me

_____ For suggestions on how to respond to homophobia and prejudice

_____ To help me be less afraid to stand up and speak out against discrimination

Gay, Bisexual, or Questioning?

Now, about this odd little acronym I'm using: GBQ. Why bother with the Q part? Including men who are questioning is very important; they form a very large percentage of this book's potential audience. Some men are still in the process of discovering whether they are gay, bisexual, or if their same-sex feelings are temporary. Some men are confused by the whole label thing; that makes them questioning, too. Some men don't consider themselves to be strictly gay, bisexual, *or* heterosexual; their sexual orientation is evolving over time. Others, impatient with categories of any sort, want to remain flexible in the way they express their love. The issue for some men is that they are attracted to a specific individual, male or female, based on some special characteristics of the person. I include all these men in the questioning category.

An issue that may be important to you is whether you want to label your sexuality at all. Some GBQ people argue (just as many heterosexuals do) that it is important to make a commitment about who you are and what you like, by putting a name to your sexuality and love interests. Many in the gay and bisexual community have lately revived the label *queer*, using it with enthusiasm in spite of its previously derogatory context. The word homosexual is now used more comfortably, as well, after years of being spat out in fear and hatred by anti-gay legislators and right-wing religious leaders, or used in cold, clinical ways by misguided clergy and disinterested medical professionals.

Whether you decide to label yourself as GBQ or not is up to you. Chapter 2 offers some guidelines for GBQ self-identification and, along with chapter 3, helps you focus on becoming comfortable with yourself no matter who you are.

Gay or Bisexual: Some Similarities and Differences

So what are some of the "apparent" similarities and differences in gays and bisexuals? Does it matter to you? You can take what's said here and discover and decide the rest for yourself. Don't overanalyze or overpersonalize this stuff. Although scientific research in the area of sexual orientation is improving and increasing, such studies have their limitations. Certainly they offer important hypotheses about general trends in human sexuality; but they didn't study *you*.

That said, let's take a look at some of the information that's been gathered. With larger numbers of bisexual and gay youth willing to come out, we are beginning to see a revolution in the way people view and accept diverse sexual orientations (Leland 1995). There also appears to be significant diversity among GBQ people being studied. For example, some people are first aware of their homoerotic feelings anywhere from a year old to their twenties and beyond (D'Augelli 1991).

How many gay and bisexual people are there in the United States? A study by the University of Chicago in 1992 (Laumann et al. 1994) estimated the following figures for "gay men":

- 2.8 percent of men identified themselves as gay or bisexual (comparable statistic for women was 1.4 percent)

- 10.1 percent exhibited same-gender sexuality in their desires, behaviors, and/or self-identification (comparable statistic for women was 8.6 percent)

- 0.7 percent of men said they had both male and female sexual partners in a twelve-month period (comparable statistic for women was 0.3 percent)

As far back as 1948, the Kinsey Institute's study of 5400 American (white) men found that 10 percent reported they were more or less exclusively homosexual for at least three years between ages sixteen and fifty-five; 50 percent said they responded erotically to other men; and 37 percent said they had had a homosexual experience that resulted in orgasm (for women, the results were 2–6 percent, 28 percent, and 13 percent, respectively).

We may never know what the exact numbers are. Some GBQ folks say, "I don't care." Others emphasize that higher numbers mean greater voice, visibility, and power for political and economic gains. Accurate counts mean a more authoritative stand to obtain parity with heterosexuals in civil and human rights (for fair housing and employment, freedom from discrimination, recognition, and the freedom to live and love as we choose).

What about the differences between gay and bisexual men? Some differences did emerge in one comparison of several studies of these two groups (Fox 1995). For example, it was reported that gay men experience their first sexual attraction toward other men two to three years before bisexual men, who experienced their first sexual attractions toward other men in their early to middle teens. This trend is similar for the act of self-identification: gay men self-identify as such two to three years earlier than bisexual men, who typically do so in their early to middle twenties.

Fox (1995) emphasizes the need for gay men to acknowledge and validate homosexual attractions and relationships to achieve a positive and integrated sexual identity. In comparison, bisexual men need to acknowledge and validate both homosexual and heterosexual aspects of their identity "regardless of the degree to which either or both of these are actualized in sexual behavior or relationships." Fox also describes a multidimensional (a little here and a lot there) versus a dichotomous (either/or) perspective in classifying sexual orientation. You will have a chance to assess this for yourself in chapter 2. Chapter 9 also discusses a few differences, as suggested by researchers, between bisexuals and gays in identity development and the coming-out process.

One important difference between gay men and bisexual men is the "visible community," and the support systems that exist for gay men but are more scarce for bisexual men (Fox 1995). Although bisexuals are now included in many community organizations, programs, and parades across the nation, specifically bisexual issues and identity often get lost in the mix with gay and lesbian groups.

Keep in mind that every individual is unique. There is not necessarily any single pattern of behaviors, relationships, or attractions within groups of men who self-identify as gay or bisexual. GBQ men may be more or less interested in same- or both-sex behavior across a spectrum, regardless of their self-identification as gay or bisexual.

Clearly there is need for substantially more research in these areas. You may want to read some of the available materials and the ever-increasing research to familiarize yourself with all the aspects of gay and bisexual comparison (Bohan 1996).

A Few Words about Women

Women may be the opposite sex, but are they really opposite from you? As a male, are you more alike than different from a female in terms of how you think, feel, and experience life? How does gender stereotyping influence what you feel about yourself as a GBQ man? Even if you are attracted exclusively to males and spend most of your time with men, pay close attention to the influence women have had in your life. Appreciate the important roles women have played in your past and present relationships, and how as a GBQ man you can continue to learn from women. Notice how women in general, and lesbians in particular, have a more difficult path to walk toward freedom and parity than GBQ men do. (Indeed, women with the same amount of education as their male counterparts still earn only about 60 percent or less of what men do for the same jobs.)

GBQ men have a lot to be thankful for with regard to the changes women have created in the world over the past several decades. The feminist movement of the 1970s and 1980s and women's ongoing struggle today for economic and political equality have had significant influence on your place in society as a GBQ man.

As you work through this book, keep in mind the importance of women to your history, your psyche (attitudes, wounds, feelings, and beliefs), and your day-to-day relationships. Women, whether it's your mother, sister, employer, friend, neighbor, girlfriend, coworker, or lover, in the past or present, are important components of your growth as a GBQ man.

How and with Whom to Share Your Coming-Out Process

Later, you'll do some work on deciding if you want to come out, to whom, how to do it, and when. But first, you need to start thinking about finding a supportive person or two who already knows you are GBQ. Your goal is to find someone who will walk with you through the coming-out and self-examination process. Coming out brings out many feelings—guilt, excitement, homophobia (yes, even in you!), the need to find relationships, reactions to prejudice and hurt, and so on. It helps to have a buddy, confidante, or counselor to share your feelings with, ask questions of, and collaborate with on your goals.

Who do you want to share your coming out process with? Find a friend, mentor, family member, or therapist with whom you can talk freely about being GBQ. Find someone willing to listen to you about what this book brings up for you, and who can give you feedback and responses to what you have to say. Your ally should be someone who can be there for you over time, walking with you on your GBQ journey (or at least until you finish this book).

Naturally, you'll want to be able to trust your support person. The two of you should share mutual respect and should value each other's opinions even when you don't agree. You may want to test the water with this person first—especially if the person is heterosexual—by discussing some gay or bisexual topics in a general way (such as legalization of same-sex marriages, gays in the military, pride parades, or a gay character in a movie). Pay attention to how the person listens and see if he or she is open to your thoughts. Notice if the person seems uncomfortable or shows any signs of disapproval. Can he or she sympathize or empathize? Do you feel safe?

Of course it's ultimatelyup to you to establish the boundaries of this alliance. Only you can decide how much you want to say and how vulnerable you are willing to feel. Be aware, however, that you may be so relieved about having someone with whom to finally discuss your sexual orientation and coming-out process that you end up wanting to share *everything*. That could leave you more open to getting hurt than you would like, and you may be frightened off by the sudden feelings of vulnerability. Even if this happens, however, you can recover and learn from the experience.

On the other hand, you may want to keep your coming-out process personal, at least for now. If complete privacy is right for you then you might consider keeping a journal of your thoughts and feelings as a way to stay in touch with all your emotions and experiences. Journaling can be a good strategy to develop yourself as an ally, which we'll talk about in chapter 5.

Answer the following questions to see if you have a coming-out confidante.

Is there someone in your life now with whom you think you'd want to share your coming-out process? Why this person?

_____

_____

_____

_____

How much do you think you're willing to share with this person? (For example: a lot, some, just a little, I'll have to see along the way)

_____

_____

_____

_____

How do you feel about being vulnerable with this person?

_____

_____

_____

_____

Keep a Journal of Your Process

Whether you decide to share your coming-out process with someone or you choose to work alone, journaling is a great way to directly track your emotional and psychological process over time. There are many opportunities in this book to put your thoughts to paper. Some of the exercises are directed at journaling. However, if in addition to reading this book you begin keeping a journal of what you think, feel, and experience as you work with your GBQ issues, you will deepen your self-understanding. Journaling will help you be more objective in observing your inner life, much as a good parent, coach, or friend would do with your behavior.

You may want to buy a notebook or journal specifically for this purpose. I encourage you to write, draw, color, cut and paste pictures, and include poetry, memories, or symbols that have heartfelt meaning to your GBQ journey. Keep your journal in a safe place and keep it confidential. If you feel you want to share your journal, do so carefully and only with those you trust. You might share with someone who knows, cares about, and/or respects your vulnerabilities. Emotional boundaries are important here as they serve to make you secure and reinforce that you will be respectful of your own needs.

Where You're Heading

The main thrust of this book is to assist you to maximize your well-being. How do you get there? One way is by honoring and integrating the different aspects of your GBQ self. *Coming Out Every Day* aims to support and challenge you by questioning what you know about yourself and what it means to be GBQ, all the while helping you to clarify the essential elements of who you are and who you want to be.

So take this opportunity to congratulate yourself for picking up this book and taking the first step in your everyday journey. Good luck!

I

Taking Your Personal Inventory

A lot of coming-out issues are similar for everyone. Some age-related issues, however, may require special consideration, for example, coming out in midlife. Specific circumstances create different issues as well: for example, if you are married, have an established career, or have been exposed to extremes such as abuse and poverty. So you will need to take your age and life experiences into account as you work through the various exercises in this book. In this chapter, you will answer questions and consider aspects of your life that will affect your GBQ journey.

Your Age and Phase of Life

This book is for all GBQ men, whether you are coming out for the first time or are well along in the process. Some discussions will contain material that is more helpful if you have been out for a number of years or are out to a lot of people—for instance, the chapters on shame, relationships, and health. If you are approaching the first steps of coming out, the material in chapters 7 to 9 will be more helpful. In terms of age, the focus is primarily on adult men; but adolescents, as well, will find much that is relevant.

Take a minute now to identify where you are in your life.

I am _____ years old.

I am _____ (not at all, a little, somewhat, very much) aware of how my age and my life circumstances make a difference to me as a GBQ man.

Coming to terms with my sexual orientation is unique for me at my age because:

_____

_____

_____

_____

What Does Coming Out Mean to You?

Take a moment to think about what coming out means to you at this time in your life. Answer the following questions:

As a GBQ man, what does the coming-out process mean to you?

_____

_____

_____

_____

As a _____ (write in any unique circumstances here, such as, father of two children; Asian American; partner in a committed relationship) and a GBQ man, the coming-out process also means

_____

_____

_____

_____

If you are HIV-positive, what does the coming-out process mean to you? (Examples: Being faced with coming out about my health; being really personal with others if I want.)

_____

_____

_____

_____

Valuable Life Experiences

Make some notes here about the life experiences you think are valuable or in some way relevant to understanding your development or coming out as a GBQ man. Just jot down a few brief comments here, because we'll be studying these subjects in detail in later chapters.

Family of origin, assigned family roles, and what I learned about sex from my family. (Examples: I was adopted; I'm an only child; I took care of my siblings and didn't learn to acknowledge my own needs; My parents drank too much; My parents were loving and supportive; Sex wasn't discussed at all in my family; Homosexuality was considered wrong.)

_____

_____

_____

_____

Abuse. (Examples: I was not abused by anyone growing up; I was physically and emotionally mistreated by kids in elementary school; I was sexually abused by my brother; My father often hit me.)

_____

_____

_____

_____

Social and academic experiences in school. (Examples: I felt "different" from the other boys in my grade; Kids picked on me; I was a loner; I knew lots of people but they didn't really know me; I did well in school and loved it; Learning disabilities made math hard for me.)

Social: _____

_____

_____

_____

Academic: _____

_____

_____

_____

Relationships with friends and lovers. (Examples: I have a few close supportive friends; I never made friends easily; I have no GBQ friends; I've been in love twice; I'm married and very much in the closet; I've dated women and have started to meet guys, but haven't had a long-term relationship; I had some crushes on men, but they never knew.)

Friends: _____

_____

_____

_____

Lovers: _____

_____

_____

_____

Sexual experiences. (Examples: Lots of experimentation with both sexes as a teen; I've never had a same-sex experience; Some anonymous sex with men; Tried to make it with women, but the passion wasn't there.)

_____

_____

_____

_____

Career. (Examples: I'm still in school and don't yet know what I want to do; I've been working in a job I like for many years; I want to change careers; I keep my personal life separate from my career; I'm out with certain people at work.)

_____

_____

_____

_____

Substance abuse. (Examples: I drink two beers a day and smoke pot on weekends; I experimented as a teen; I don't drink at all; I drink too much now; I'm clean and sober; I use alcohol to deal with GBQ feelings.)

_____

_____

_____

Personal growth. (Examples: I'm in therapy; I've never discussed my sexual orientation; I'm discussing my sexual orientation now in a support group; This is my first experience of really looking at myself in this way.)

_____

_____

_____

_____

Other. (Examples: I'm a father; My religious background doesn't allow for being gay or bisexual; My race and sexuality create possibilities for double stigma.)

_____

_____

_____

_____

Go back to the items you listed and put an X by the negative ones—the ones you think interfere with your development as a healthy GBQ man. Put a star by the positive ones—those you think helped or will help your coming-out process as a GBQ man. Think about the items you've marked and about the ones you feel neutral about.

In the space below, write a little about how you want to deal with the negative influences and how you want to use the neutral and positive influences in your GBQ maturation and journey. Again, be brief—this exercise is a jumping-off point for future exercises, so don't worry about being too detailed.

In terms of the negative influences on my GBQ development, I would like to: (Examples: stop letting other's opinions of me get in the way of being openly gay/bi and happy; eliminate the influence and contact with abusive/disrespectful people; find a group of friends who are comfortable knowing me as a gay/bi man.)

_____

_____

_____

_____

In terms of the neutral and positive influences on my GBQ development, I would like to: (Examples: use my past sexual experiences to find a person who meets my needs for sex *and* intimacy; remain clean and sober; keep working on standing up for myself, especially in homophobic situations.)

Special Considerations

GBQ men have to contend with considerable societal fear and prejudice toward their sexual orientation. In addition to these concerns, some GBQ men have special considerations, such as life circumstances, abilities, cultures, religious backgrounds, and limitations. Although this book aims to be relevant across cultures and to all GBQ men, you will need to be sensitive to your own special circumstances and needs as you answer the questions in each chapter.

Now let's look at these areas of special consideration. You may want to make notes in your journal or on a separate piece of paper to help focus your efforts as you work through the exercises in this book.

Marriage

If you're currently married and just now coming out to yourself, you will probably need to make some critical decisions. If you have not already done so, consider picking a moment to have a discussion with your wife about your sexuality. First, though, you may want to consult a GBQ-sensitive therapist who can assist you with your feelings and help you sort out what to say and how to talk with your spouse. It's unfair to continue keeping this secret about yourself from a person who has signed on to be your equal partner in life. Of course you will be faced with her confusion, anger, pain, and reproach. Yes, the relationship may come to an end. But for any relationship to succeed, it's essential to share an issue that so directly affects the other party.

Try to be empathetic to your wife's situation. How would you feel in her position? What you have to say can be traumatic for her, in that the old you (or perhaps the you she thought she knew) has changed irrevocably. Your truth will feel as hurtful to her as if you were telling her that you are having an affair with another, yet it may be more difficult for her to understand because of the same-sex aspect of your attractions. Were you in her position, however, it's likely you'd prefer to know the truth and be given the opportunity to respond with all the facts on the table. Give her the same respect.

Your wife may already have an inkling that you're GBQ, which may make coming out to her a relief for you both. But even if she thinks she knows, or you think she knows, you should still give her the respect she deserves by telling her the truth. If you are sexually active and "unsafe" outside your marriage, you could be risking the possibility of unknowingly exposing yourself and your wife to HIV and other sexually transmitted diseases.

In the event you want to stay married, your wife must be part of this decision—it isn't only up to you. Many women do decide they still want to try to make it work, even though their husbands are gay or bisexual. Your wife may try to change you. She might say she is willing to "share you" with men; but if you're tempted to stay married while experimenting on the side, think seriously about what the two of you are agreeing to. Consider your motivations for wanting to retain the status quo (say, for emotional or financial security, for the kids, because you're best friends, and so on). Clinical experience suggests that in general, gay and bisexual men who stay married under such circumstances are poor risks for continued marital success. Both partners in a marriage where the man is GBQ soon grow weary of the man's divided loyalties. Jealousy and other forms of anger may become debilitating.

Your personal development as a GBQ man depends on your ability to honestly explore your sexuality outside of typical heterosexual marital contracts. GBQ men coming to grips with their feelings often need ample opportunity to emotionally and sexually explore their needs, wants, identities, and new relationships. Such exploration is not conducive to the stability and commitment of heterosexual marriage. You may think, "Well, we're different!" But you're also human, both of you—and you both have inner needs and feelings that must be considered.

Some couples *are* different and do find ways to make it work. However, you must do some deep personal examination as to whether remaining in your marriage will work. Try to keep communication open between you and your wife. If you remain conflicted about whether to stay in the marriage, take the time to consult with a psychotherapist who is familiar with these issues, or join a support group with men in similar situations. Your wife, too, should search out similar support groups. Read some of the books that address this topic in greater detail (see the resources section).

Parenting

If you're a father, coming out to your child (or children) can be a challenge for all involved—you, the child's mother, and the child. As a GBQ dad, you may be concerned about how your child views you, how being out may expose your child to prejudice, or that your child may not be able to understand what it means to be GBQ. Working through the exercises in this book can help you achieve the confidence you need to deal with the issues GBQ fathers must face.

The developmental stage and maturity level of your child, as well as how you approach dealing with your sexual orientation, factor in to how your child adjusts. As a general rule of thumb, the more comfortable and natural you are with your orientation, and the younger your child is when he or she is exposed to your GBQ status as "just a part of who dad is," the easier the child's adjustment will be. Keep in mind, however, that there are, of course, exceptions to every rule.

Consider your personal experiences and issues as a father as you work through the exercises. You may also want to check out some of the specific books for GBQ fathers listed in the resources section.

Personality

This book takes into account many styles of personality and differences in the way people relate to one another. For example, if you are a shy person you will get an opportunity to look at how your shyness will affect your coming-out process and how you will respond to it. The exercises give you ample opportunity to explore who you are, what you like and don't like about your style, and how you might change your responses. Chapter 3, for example, contains discussion and exercises concerning defensive obstacles and personality patterns that may get in the way of expressing yourself and growing in healthy ways as a GBQ man.

If you suspect that you have significant personality problems (for example, a pattern of rigidity and inflexibility, problems taking responsibility for your behavior, a history of unstable relationships), you may want to use Coming Out Every Day in conjunction with psychotherapy. Whatever your personality obstacles, you should work through the sections of this book at your own pace; try not to compare your coming-out process with others' and ask for help from a therapist or other support person if you find yourself getting stuck.

Mental Health

You can't read a self-help book today that doesn't have improving your psychological well-being as one of its goals. Here, too, that is a primary issue, and this book will help you take major steps in that direction.

Yet, many folks have special mental health needs that make self-help more challenging. If you have struggled with special issues of mental health, you'll need to acknowledge these difficulties as you begin or continue coming out. These special issues include moderate to serious clinical depression (not just the occasional blues, but chronic sadness); bouts of mania; psychotic symptoms; and anxiety disorders such as panic attacks or post-traumatic stress disorder. Be patient and make allowances for the amount of time necessary to make changes and meet your goals when working through the exercises. It is stressful enough to work through issues of shame, identity, and relationships with a GBQ orientation, without suffering from complications that a psychological disorder can bring about. Regardless, don't compare yourself with others who might be working through their GBQ struggles in ways different from you.

Support and counseling will be invaluable to you if you have mental health issues. The guidance of a GBQ-affirmative therapist, or the group support of other GBQ men struggling with mental health problems, will likely be useful in helping you work through your coming-out process.

Culture and Ethnicity

Your culture has been passed down to you through many generations and has many aspects to it. It is your ethnic and religious beliefs and values, your manners, your family myths and celebrations, gender roles, language patterns, the music you dance to, and much more. And it is also, of course, what you learn about sex and love.

Even in the turmoil of our rapidly changing global village, you carry with you certain customs and aspects of your culture that influence the ways you incorporate your sexuality into your everyday identity. For example, you may have grown up in a culture that believes real men don't cry—men are supposed to be tough, not sensitive; that showing affection toward and loving another man is wrong; or that boys should like sports.

How do you think your culture of origin has influenced your feelings about being a GBQ man?

_____

_____

_____

_____

Are you now living in a cultural environment different from the one in which you were raised? How does this environment help or hinder your search for well-being as a GBQ man?

_____

_____

_____

_____

Your ethnic heritage, too, is an important consideration in your experience with this book. Let's take an objective and dispassionate look at why this is so.

In the United States, the dominant culture has historically been white-influenced. The white, Christian, heterosexual man of European heritage has composed the major ethnic group in most parts of this country for generations. In terms of actual numbers, so-called minority groups may in fact be the larger population; however, the most significant power base is white. This undeniable fact means that most of the research done about gay and bisexual men has primarily involved white males.

What does this mean for you if your racial origin is African American, Asian, Pacific Islander, Latino, or another racial group? Or if you have grown up in a disenfranchised or oppressed population or geographical area? It means that some of what you experience in this book will need to be tailored to your personal specifications. Throughout the book, especially chapter 13, I have incorporated information that focuses on racial and ethnic differences that may have an impact on the discussion. As you read, I'll often remind you to pay attention to the influences of your ethnic circumstances.

If you are a GBQ man of color, it's likely you have experienced double stigmatization (Gonsiorek 1995). Your struggle is twofold: not only are you GBQ, but you are a member of a group that does not have significant power in American society. You may feel like more of an outcast from general society than other GBQ men, and your self-esteem may be further hurt by the censure from your own ethnic group.

If you are a GBQ man of color, exactly what allowances should you make as you work through this book? First and foremost, you need to be aware of your differences as you read each chapter. Pay attention to how your membership in an emerging group influences your identity development. Ask yourself if issues such as shame and stigmatization are more intense for you than what is discussed in this book. The adjustments you make for your ethnic and cultural status will make your experience with this book more profound, deepening and strengthening your GBQ self-help process.

Mental and Physical Challenges

If you are physically or mentally challenged, your approach to this book may also be different. Sensory challenges, such as sight or hearing impairments, or physical challenges resulting from military experience, birth defects, or accidents mean that you also suffer stigmatization in our society.

Men with learning challenges, who perhaps can't read well, have an attention-deficit disorder, or have difficulty processing information or thinking abstractly, suffer greatly in our society. If you are one of these men, you may have been stigmatized from an early age in school and at home. Most of the world still unfairly thinks of you as "an exception" rather than exceptional. Like GBQ men of color, you must deal with this disapprobation in addition to that of being GBQ. Whether the stigma and suffering came first from your early feelings of being GBQ or from your other special issues may be hard to discern. Nevertheless, the sum of the pain can be greater than its individual sources.

No matter what your mental or physical challenge, it's critical that you give yourself the opportunities to be your personal best. Most GBQ men can relate to stigma of any kind and what it means to be different. And the inclusion of mentally or physically challenged men in the GBQ mix contributes to our diversity. Keep these things in mind if you find yourself losing faith in yourself and your abilities as a GBQ man. Incorporate your unique experiences as you work through the exercises in this book.

HIV

HIV and AIDS are discussed as special coming-out considerations in chapter 8 and as health considerations in chapter 12. If you are HIV-positive, you must pay attention to the impact of your status on all dimensions of your well-being. You, like others whose health is compromised by stress or illness, have to work harder than other guys to maximize your energy and feel your best.

As you work through this book, be alert to special problems you may experience as a result of your HIV status. You will want to focus on how your status figures into issues of self-esteem, shame and guilt, dating and relationships, and on the coming-out process in general. You may also need special support and counseling. HIV affects everyone in today's world, not just GBQ folks. Learn how to talk about it and how to be honest, at least to yourself, about all of your GBQ needs.

Launching into Your GBQ Process

Take a piece of paper and fold it in half. You'll need a pencil and possibly some colored pencils or pens.

On the outside of the paper, draw, write, or color a representation of what you show about yourself to the outside world (family, friends, colleagues, and so on). You may want to draw yourself or include any feelings, symbols, or colors that represent what you share and show to others. Next, open the paper, and on the inside, draw a representation of what you don't show, or what you hide and keep secret from others—certain emotions, thoughts, or aspects of your self. As with the outside, you may want to use colors, symbols, or words.

How different or the same are the two sides of the paper? How would you like to change this? What would it be like to have your outside self more closely match your inside self, especially as a GBQ man?

_____

_____

_____

_____

Before you go any further, take a minute to write, sketch, or visualize your concerns, hopes, dreams, and aspirations for integrating your inside and outside selves and for your personal experience in general with _Coming Out Every Day._

_____

_____

_____

_____

_____

_____

_____

_____

_____

Well, you've examined the structure of this book and should know a little of what to expect. You've also taken your personal inventory and sketched out your first version of some goals to work towards as a GBQ man. So, let's get started.

2

Who Am I?

This above all: to thine own self be true,
And it must follow, as the night the day,
Thou canst not be false to any man.

—William Shakespeare, *Hamlet*

Now that you've familiarized yourself with the direction of this book, here in chapter 2 you'll get a chance to explore the various forms of your identity, clarify your sexual orientation, appreciate your uniqueness, and stretch your personal "comfort zones."

Real Self versus False Self

Larry, a gay man in his thirties, always fell short of feeling good about his accomplishments. He consistently worked too much, fearful that he would be judged as flaky, inadequate, or unintelligent. He always occupied himself with one task after another because he was anxious about being alone. He was either aloof or passive and never really felt comfortable around others. Larry had developed a false self that kept away painful feelings, avoided the realities of life, and never allowed him to achieve a healthy, whole self. He had not learned to acknowledge the positive *and* negative aspects of his emotions and self.

The concept of real and false selves is a fascinating one that has been used in the study of object relations and self-psychology. I will be using these terms somewhat loosely, rather than in their strictest psycho-logical definition. The real-self-versus-false-self concept is something that many GBQ men can sink their teeth into. It helps them find ways to embrace a healthy, integrated gay or bisexual identity.

Here are the basics of real-versus-false self:

- The real self faces reality, no matter how upsetting it is; the false self avoids reality.

- The real self puts its unique desires and qualities first; the false self tries to fit in and be liked at all costs.

- The false self is confused, depressed, and anxious about the dif-ferent roles you play in life.

- When the real self says, "I am one person, growing, changing, and shifting with many roles," the false self believes you are a phony.

- The real self acknowledges you are not perfect and wants to learn from mistakes.

- The real self is willing to deal with tough times.

- The real self is accepting; the false self is defensive.

- The real self trusts who you are and what you do, even when you're unsure about something; the false self does not trust.

- The real self nurtures, soothes, and supports; the false self sabo-tages.

- The real self is flexible but stable. The real self takes the stance of "I know who I am, but I'm willing to consider my (and your) changing wants and needs"; the false self is rigid and uncom-fortable.

GBQ men are particularly vulnerable to developing a false self. As a GBQ man, you may need the false self as a protective mask that pro-vides comfort from painful feelings of rejection, aloneness, shame or guilt, humiliation, and actual physical harm. The false self for a GBQ man is often a defense against threats to feeling okay about being who he is.

You may have developed a false self not just out of your experience with uncomfortable feelings or experiences related to your sexuality. You will want to look at all the different ways you have blocked your real self from growth; for example, you may be avoiding your feelings due to a general feeling of being unlovable—not just because you're a GBQ man. For our purposes, however, the next group of exercises will help you examine how, as a GBQ man, you have stifled your real self in regards to your sexual orientation. You'll see how you can support your real self, instead, to stay focused on maintaining a healthy wholeness.

Unfortunately, as a GBQ man you may have "split off" from your real self, leaving behind your feelings of love, passion, and uniqueness. This split for you may come in the form of "trying to be straight;" avoiding or masking feelings of potential attraction to certain people; or hiding any "differentness" in your appearance, feelings, thoughts, and actions.

Getting to Know Your Selves

List your attitudes, actions, and beliefs that you think have more to do with your false self, and those that come from your real self. You may want to ask yourself what feelings you hide or how you avoid being true to yourself. I've supplied a couple of examples to get you started.

False Self	**Real Self**
_____ *Avoiding being responsible for my actions*	_____ *Admitting to my same-sex attractions*
_____ *Pretending everything is all right, when it's really not*	_____ *Talking about my anger honestly*

In the False Self column, put a check mark beside those qualities that are related to hiding or trying to cope with being GBQ.

In the Real Self column, put a star beside those qualities that help you to be more congruous and allow you to grow as GBQ man. These are the ways you can continue to support your real self. If you haven't listed any such qualities, think of some and add them to the list. Dropping the defenses of your false self may take some persistence, but will become considerably more effortless as you support your coming-out process, and discover and promote the real parts of your gay or bisexual self.

Write in the spaces below the names of specific people in your life (past and present) who have and can continue to support your real self as a GBQ man.

Parent(s) _____

Sibling(s) _____

Friend(s) _____

Colleague(s) _____

Acquaintance(s) _____

Teacher(s) _____

Other(s) _____

Finding Himself

Thom has known he had gay feelings since he was six, when he "fell in love" with the guy next door. Though loving, his parents were strict in their religious principles. Peers made fun of Thom's interests in "soft stuff" like reading, playing house, and music; he didn't like the rough-and-tumble play of most boys his age and was typically left out of recess and PE activities. His real self was sensitive, gentle, and enthusiastic, but over the years he had developed a demeanor that was "tough" and somewhat distant. He didn't let people in easily. As a young adult he had a great deal of trouble believing in himself, getting close with other people, and admitting his mistakes. At the same time, he was beginning to acknowledge his same-sex feelings. He had split off these feelings and desires, afraid of ridicule and mistreatment from others. He was living a lie—safe, but unhappy and unfulfilled. Thom sought help and found a gay-affirming psychotherapist. Together they worked at keeping Thom on track with his real-self goals, while recognizing and dealing with his fearful false self at the same time.

Think of strategies you can use to remain committed to your real self. Examples might be developing and using a real-self mantra ("Ommmm ... Speak my truth ... ommmm") or writing down a list of real-self goals and putting it up on the bathroom mirror so you can catch yourself and redirect your thoughts and actions when you start to drift into being "fake."

_____

_____

_____

_____

The Evolving Self

What is an *evolving self*? An evolving self suggests continuous growth and change and allows you to be true to your real self as you move through the different phases of your life.

> *The only thing that one really knows about human nature is that*
> *it changes. Change is the one quality, we can predicate on it.*
>
> —Oscar Wilde

The Developmental Life Cycle

Psychologists, therapists, and sociologists have given a name to life's changes: the *developmental life cycle*. It is a part of growing up and growing old. The cycle has various physical, psychological, and social stages—from infancy to old age, and everything in between. You may have your own terms for these phases, such as "sowing your wild oats," "the prime of my life," or "the aches and pains stage."

Where are you now in your psychological life cycle? Do you feel that you are in between two stages or experiencing more than one stage?

Use the following lines to write your definition of your current position in the life cycle, according to your sense of yourself and the development challenges you're working on. For example, Larry wrote this definition: "At thirty-four, it's a mixed bag. I feel like I'm an adolescent because I'm finally starting to date people I'm really into and attracted to, but it feels like midlife on my job and in the house I've been living in for ten years."

_____

_____

_____

_____

In Western culture, the social developmental life cycle is often categorized in terms of the family cycle that people go through—from being single to getting married, having children, perhaps getting divorced, raising children, and so on. This particular cycle is a culturally bound, heterosexually determined developmental life cycle. Let's work on a different view of the social life cycle.

What do you think are the major differences between the traditionally defined social developmental life cycle and your own social life cycle as a GBQ individual? Also, what are your personal wants for a gay or bisexual family or system? Here's Larry's response: "I didn't feel safe to date people of my own sex as a teen and felt I had to pretend I wanted sex with girls. I think that made me act more reserved than I really am. It also made me feel that I couldn't have children unless I had a wife. What I really want is to have children in the near future and yet be in a same-sex marriage."

What do you think are the major transitions you have had through life so far, are currently having, or will have that make being a GBQ man unique (either unique to you or as compared to heterosexual men)? Larry's major transitions were, "coming out as a gay man to my parents and friends, having to hide who I am with certain people at work, and having to deal with extra prejudice because of my race."

Your Life Structure

In addition to looking at a developmental life cycle, you may also find it helpful to study your *life structure* (Levinson 1986), which is determined by your answer to the question, "What is my life like now?" Knowing your life structure is just as important as defining where you are and how you feel about your *meta-self* (where you are in the developmental life cycle process). It may help you to clarify how you accept yourself, what you want to change, and how you feel about yourself right now.

Life structure goes beyond the big picture of your current position in the developmental life cycle. Examining your life structure means examining parts of yourself, such as

- Your current physical condition and appearance
- Developmental milestones you have accomplished or are struggling with
- Your views of self, others, and life

- Your current personality traits (dominant, assertive, warm, and so on)
- Your interpersonal relations
- Your current historical context (what's happening politically, socially, ethnically)

Think of your life structure as a way to gauge the transitions of your life as a GBQ man.

What is your current life structure in terms of the areas mentioned?

_____

_____

_____

_____

Keeping in mind some of the areas listed, what do you think and how do you feel about your current life structure as a GBQ man? Are you satisfied or unsatisfied with particular aspects?

_____

_____

_____

_____

What do you want your life structure to be like in

Six months? _____

_____

_____

_____

One year? _____

_____

_____

_____

Five years? _____

_____

_____

_____

No rules or rituals have been sanctioned and given legitimacy for GBQ boys and men to follow. This is not to say you're all alone in the world without any examples—many gay, bisexual, and questioning men throughout history have had to find their own way. Like you, they have had to try to understand and acknowledge their nontraditional developmental life cycles and life structures. After completing the last several exercises in defining where you are in these life cycles, you are somewhat closer to your real self as a GBQ man, despite the probability that pieces of your self from the past may have been hidden, repressed, or oppressed. And you can come back to these exercises as many times as you need to, to gain even more insight into who you are and how you're evolving.

You may want to check out your local bookstore or take a look at some of the gay history books included in this book's references list. Read up on what others have done as they made their way down the avenues of gay and bisexual life.

The Many Faces of Identity

Your social, gender, sexual, and love identities are four essential features of who you are. The challenge for you as a GBQ man is to really know and be yourself—despite past admonitions you may have received to do exactly the opposite. Now, let's get to know the multiple facets of your identity.

Social Identity

Most individuals, no matter what their ethnic or cultural background, perform diverse and multiple roles in life. Think of these roles as characteristic and expected social behavior in your life. As a GBQ man, you have many *choices* for defining who you are—to yourself and to others in your world. In the upcoming exercise, you'll look at the unique roles you play in your own life so you can begin to see where you are in your developmental life process. Then, in the two subsequent exercises, you'll also get an idea of how "out" you may want to be in your different roles about your same-sex desires.

Make a Role List

First, clarify who you are in terms of your various social roles by naming the different roles you perform in your current life. You might include friend, son, employee, parent, athlete, lover, student, and others. It may help to imagine the roles you typically assume at certain times, such as on weekdays, weekends, and holidays. You also perform roles in the activities you participate in—hobbies and sports, for instance—and in certain settings, such as work, home, and so on.

List as many roles as you can think of.

_____	_____
_____	_____
_____	_____
_____	_____
_____	_____

Study Your Roles

The roles you've just identified are a part of your *external* self and behavior—the way you show yourself to others. Obviously there are many other parts to your identity. In addition to these external roles, you have an *internal* self—your feelings, thoughts, and fantasies. How deeply you know that internal self is up to you. It depends on your openness and honesty and the limits of your awareness. Men, in particular, are used to describing themselves based on what they *do*, rather than on what they think and feel. One of the ultimate goals of this book is to help you become more familiar and comfortable with your internal self and then integrate the external and internal selves.

In the past you may have struggled with integrating your internal and external selves for a lot of reasons. Many individuals—heterosexual, bisexual, and gay—want to be more aware of their inner life. They want to find peace through some sort of integration of their feelings with the reality and consistency of their external life. As a GBQ man, your goal is to have your internal world (feelings, sexual desires and fantasies, loves, interests, values) more closely match your external world (your choice of whom you love and desire, your sexual activities, your friends, and the way you show and share yourself as you're performing all your roles) in order to create a true whole-person identity.

GBQ men who have been scorned by society and even themselves may have particular difficulty with addressing their feelings of love and passion, as well as their erotic thoughts and fantasies about other men. In one way or another, these thoughts and feelings may not have been expressed or shared on the outside and may have become split off from your whole-person identity. You may have learned to segregate the parts of yourself that are considered "objectionable" by people close to you, or by society in general.

Complete the following chart to compare what you show to the outside world with what you don't show. Consider the roles you iden- tified above. As you walk through these roles and relationships, what do you show about yourself and what do you hide from the outside world? Included as examples are a couple of items on Craig's list.

The Role I Play	What I Show	What I Hide
Craig the athlete	*Love of sports; a healthy body*	*Attraction to men*
Craig the son	*Caring for parents*	*Who I'm dating*
_____	_____	_____
	_____	_____
	_____	_____
_____	_____	_____
	_____	_____
	_____	_____
_____	_____	_____
	_____	_____
	_____	_____
_____	_____	_____
	_____	_____
	_____	_____
_____	_____	_____
	_____	_____
	_____	_____
_____	_____	_____
	_____	_____
	_____	_____
_____	_____	_____
	_____	_____
	_____	_____
_____	_____	_____
	_____	_____

Armed with clearer knowledge of the roles in your life, and the aspects of yourself that you hide or reveal as a GBQ man, you'll be better able to interpret your internal self. You have probably figured out by now that what you show often differs significantly from what you hide. The extent of this difference depends on how open and comfortable you are about yourself and your sexual orientation, which you'll work on in later chapters.

Gender Identity

Uninformed (and in some cases, mean-spirited) people sometimes refer to GBQ men as having "gender identity confusion." In truth, *gender identity* has nothing to do with sexual orientation. Gender identity is your own male or female essence and is not necessarily about biology. Transgendered individuals, for example, often feel that internally they're of a different gender than what is indicated by their sex organs, body types, and genes.

You have certain bodily characteristics and mannerisms that identify you as a man. While your social roles and interests contribute to your male identity to a certain degree, they can be considered separate from your gender identity and called your *gender role*.

Who Are You As a Man?

To begin the process of examining your gender identity, complete the following statements about yourself. Keep your answers specific to gender characteristics, male roles, and interests (as you define them). Don't judge; later we'll come back to what you like and don't like about yourself, inside and out.

In general, what makes me feel like a man is

_____

_____

My dominant masculine characteristics are

_____

_____

My dominant feminine characteristics are

_____

_____

I would like to change the following about the way I express my masculinity:

_____

_____

I would like to change the following about the way I express my femininity:

_____

_____

Sexual Identity

Sexual identity describes what you like sexually, and whom you are passionate about. As you work through this section, don't get caught in the label trap by saying "I'm bisexual" or "I'm gay"—we will sort that out later in this chapter. Bear in mind that sexual identity is not only what you do on the outside; it's also who and what turns you on.

Here you will want to consider your sexual fantasies and favorite themes. For example, you may be specifically turned on by certain physical characteristics of men and/or women—facial features, height, body shape, and so on. In personality and behavioral characteristics, your turn-on may be your partner's assertiveness or shyness, talkativeness or serenity, rational thinking patterns or impetuosity, and the like. The sexual acts that excite you may be oral sex, rubbing, kissing, and so on. List what turns you on in a partner—who the partner is and what the partner does.

In terms of physical characteristics, I like a partner who

_____

_____

In terms of personality and behavior, what really turns me on sexually is a partner who is

_____

_____

My most sexually passionate feelings usually involve (include gender and specific qualities, as well as specific acts and fantasies)

_____

_____

Love Identity

Your *love identity* may or may not be the same as your sexual identity.

Imagine that you're on an island with just one other person who will be with you as your partner for the rest of your life. Think and feel for a moment about the qualities that you need your partner to contribute to your loving relationship as you both grow older.

Although some of this may change as you grow, you will be able to identify some themes that have existed for significant parts of your current life, and in years past, as well. For example, you may want your partner to be both compassionate and rational about life during difficult times, or to be open to physical affection and play. You may need a partner who can be silly sometimes and yet enjoy making tough decisions together.

Again, remember that your loving feelings may be the same as, different from, or somehow related to what your erotic feelings are. Therefore, what you define as *loving* often includes the sexual as well as the emotional and passionate aspects of your love identity.

In terms of personality and behavior, I love a partner who

_____

_____

My most warm, loving feelings usually involve (include the person's gender and qualities, as well as specific acts and fantasies)

_____

_____

How, if at all, do your answers here compare with your answers in the sexual identity section? What does this tell you about yourself?

_____

_____

Gay, Bi, Questioning, or Confused: Examining Your Sexual Orientation

Now that you have looked inside at four possible ways you can identify yourself, let's give some time to fitting these parts into an actual sexual orientation. *Sexual orientation* brings together the concepts of your sexual identity and your love identity. Some people believe sexual orientation is synonymous with sexual identity, but I believe the term sexual orientation is more comprehensive and accurate.

The problem with using sexual identity is that it implies your whole identity is based primarily on sex. Orientation, however, implies what your sexual life is directed toward. I suppose sex-love orientation is an even better descriptor, but that's why we use the words gay and lesbian—to point to both love and sexual interest.

In this section, you'll have a chance to think about yourself and your sexual orientation from a multidimensional perspective and you'll examine your orientation and your coming out as a continuous lifetime process.

Once you get used to it, seeing yourself as a three-dimensional individual enriches your inner experience. It's a perspective that makes room for some creativity, letting you define yourself without the constraints of labels placed on you by others or accumulated over years of set behavior that may confuse you or may not really fit you as an individual.

At first, this multidimensional perspective may be a bit unsettling, because coming out means getting used to a new idea: the possibility that your attractions and preferences may change over time. You may go from confusion to a bisexual identity to a primarily gay orientation, or from a gay orientation to a bisexual orientation, and so on—with possibilities in between.

Although the idea of an evolving and changing sexuality may be uncomfortable for you, I encourage you to remain open to the possibility that you can discover new ways to view your orientation. On the other hand, this new perspective may give you a more solid sense of yourself as a gay or bisexual man.

Using the chart below, adapted from the Klein Sexual Orientation Grid (Klein 1985), enter an M (Men), a W (Women), or a B (Both) in the Past, Present, and Goal columns for each element of sexual orientation. For example, in terms of physical attraction, you'd enter a letter in each column to show what your attraction *mostly* was in the past, what it *mostly* is now, and what is your goal. (By goal, I mean what you want and hope for in the future—not what your parents or others would want for you.)

Sexual Orientation Areas	Past	Present	Goal
Physical attraction			
Sexual behavior			
Sexual fantasies			
Emotional preference			
Social preference			
Self-identification			
Hetero/bi/gay culture			

Now complete this statement about yourself:

This exercise has helped me to clarify that my sexual orientation

- In the past, was primarily _____

- In the present, is _____

- In the future, will most likely be _____

Identifying and Accepting Your Individuality

I can't emphasize enough that one of the most important aspects of coming to terms with yourself is coming to terms with your own *specialness* and *uniqueness*. Even if you are an identical twin with genetics exactly like your sibling's, you still possess unique personality qualities, interests, and talents that make you like no one else in the world.

As a gay, bisexual, or questioning man you are bucking an age-old assumption that to be interested in someone of the same sex means there is something unusual about you. Now I argue that being unusual is *good*—but, of course, too many of us carry around the feeling that we somehow have never and won't ever fit in to the group of humans commonly referred to as "men."

Take a moment to answer the following questions:

In what ways have I felt different because of my sexual orientation?

_____

_____

_____

_____

What have I gained by "feeling different" in my life?

_____

_____

_____

_____

What have I lost?

_____

_____

_____

_____

What was the most difficult part about feeling different or unique?

_____

_____

_____

_____

What was the best part?

_____

_____

_____

_____

If you think about it for a minute, your uniqueness has brought you both pain and pleasure. Unfortunately, it may have brought more pain than pleasure. As a result, uniqueness becomes associated with negative feelings generated by ignorance, discrimination, and your own shame.

GBQ men often reveal in therapy that, as boys, they learned to hide significant parts of themselves for fear of being labeled "different." But hiding their inner selves created a false sense of security because they were often compromising aspects of themselves. By trying so hard to belong, they closed off many truly wonderful qualities.

Try listing your special qualities. You can do it now, or over the next few days. Make a promise to yourself to find ways of appreciating your unique qualities as a GBQ man.

My unique qualities are

_____

_____

_____

_____

Here's what I like about my unique qualities:

_____

_____

_____

_____

Avoiding Stereotypes—
Negative **and** Positive

A major block to appreciating your uniqueness is buying into the stereotypes that have too often kept gay and bisexual men from viewing their sexual orientation in affirming ways. Stereotypes limit your individual experience and personal expression. This applies to both "positive" stereotypes (gay men are "neat"; bisexual men are "open-minded") and negative stereotypes (gay men are "sissies"; bisexual men are "promiscuous"). Stereotypes of both kinds are unnecessary and may be hurtful models that restrict you from being true to your unique self.

Note: Keep in mind that what defines a negative or positive stereotype for you depends on your own subjective experience.

List the *negative* stereotypes about gay or bisexual men that you have heard, seen, or read.

_____

_____

_____

_____

What *positive* stereotypes about gay or bisexual men have you heard, seen, or read?

_____

_____

_____

_____

Go back over the positive and negative stereotypes you've listed, and check the ones you think apply to the person you are now. How do these stereotypes—negative *and* positive—limit you or get in the way of feeling okay about yourself as a special and unique person?

_____

_____

_____

_____

Write down at least one way you can recognize, and then "red flag" or stop these negative or positive stereotypes from limiting you.

_____

_____

_____

_____

How you can replace the stereotypes with your own self-affirming, unique qualities? (You may want to go back to the previous section and look at what you listed for your special qualities.)

_____

_____

_____

_____

A Stereotype Story

Josh was in his early twenties during the first stages of his coming out as a gay man. He lived in San Francisco and worked with a number of gay men. It was a double-edged sword for him: on one side, he now had the opportunity to be around gay men, on the other hand, he began to compare himself with them to see how he was alike or different. Josh was sure he didn't want to be a clone of some of the guys he met. Nor did he want to be like the negative stereotypes about gay men (butch or fem, superficial, promiscuous, and so on). He wanted to just *be*. It was excruciating for him to try to define himself as a specific sexual orientation when he didn't think of himself as "one of them."

Josh realized he was reacting to many years of fear and negative judgments about himself and other gay people—judgments from friends and family, but mostly from himself. No one had ever told him, "It's okay to be who you are *and* be gay." Slowly, he started to have fun with some of the guys he had avoided because of those negative judgments. He got to know other gay men, moving beyond his preconceptions about their values and interests. And, most importantly, Josh gave himself permission to be himself and to create his own unique identity and social interests based on who he was *and* who he wanted to be.

Describe some of the ways in which you are different from the negative stereotypes.

_____

_____

_____

_____

Complete this sentence: I am a unique gay, bisexual, or questioning man because

_____

_____

_____

_____

Another Take on Stereotypes

Here's a question to get you thinking: What about those negative stereotypes—are they *really* negative? For example, take the ideas that "gay men are effeminate" and "bisexual men are just ambivalent and afraid of commitment." What's wrong with ambivalence and effeminate qualities?

Buying into stereotypes keeps you from finding out that you can be yourself without confining yourself to any "type." Your feelings of disapproval most often are due to other people's (or your own) fear of differentness, as well as insecurity about the unknown. If you were to *reframe* some of your stereotypes by separating the quality or behavior from the judgment, you might be able to refine some of those qualities that previously had a painful sting. A common example of this comes up with some gay men who realize that although they want to be more "masculine" in some of their behaviors, it's their "feminine" or sensitive qualities that allow them to access their emotions, be more intuitive, and communicate more effectively. They may decide that they will never be *truly* masculine, when in actuality, they will never be *stereotypically* masculine.

Also, remind yourself that you don't have to be liked by everyone; nor do you have to like everyone. Imagine feeling good about yourself as the unique GBQ man you are, regardless of what stereotypes you fit or what others expect you to be. This approach will stop you from negatively judging your actions or worrying about what others think of you. The need to be liked by others will be further addressed in chapter 3.

Reframed Stereotypes

Reframing stereotypes will help you positively reinforce your good feelings about yourself as the unique GBQ man you are. Your next task is to *rewrite* those negatively stereotyped qualities you identified on page 39. Rephrase them in a way that gives value to your uniqueness. For instance, jot down a few ways in which you benefit from "campy" or exaggerated feminine behaviors. Maybe you find this "humorous, and a fun way to connect with other gay men."

_____

_____

_____

_____

Finally, go back to page 39 and cross out the negative stereotypes that you want to reject as judgments about yourself.

Solidifying the Self

Now, with the various aspects of your identity and uniqueness in mind, it's time to look at how your sexual orientation is relevant to you as a whole person. When working with gay or bisexual clients, some therapists (especially heterosexual therapists in training) often make two mistakes: They either consider their client's sexual orientation as having a relationship to *everything* in the client's life, or they completely ignore sexual orientation as an issue.

While you are definitely more than your sexual orientation, it is intimately connected to your whole being. It's part of your self, your loves, your roles, your social interests, your fantasies, and your uniqueness—past, present, and future.

Gary is a forty-four-year-old man who came to therapy to discuss his bisexuality and twenty-year-marriage to his wife. He soon found that by denying his erotic interests in and continuing friendships with men, he was cutting off an important aspect of himself. He began to realize that he had also given up other parts of himself by not engaging in his usual activities, including playing an instrument in a symphony orchestra and forming closer relationships to men he liked and shared interests with. His internal self was incomplete, and he had been on shaky ground for some time. He desperately needed to acknowledge his interests, to himself and to his wife. Only by making room for more of those interests in his life, could he begin to feel truly whole and grounded. With the support of his therapist, Gary decided to talk to his wife about

Identity or Choice?

You may be sensitive to the issue of whether your sexual orientation is a choice, a biological fact, or some combination thereof. If you are like most people, your inner experience of sexual orientation is something you do not actively choose, per se. You will explore the issues of biology and choice in chapter 7.

It may be a good idea to remind yourself that your goals are evolving; they change as you change. They grow with your growing understanding of yourself, your desires, and your place in the world around you. This does not mean though that your inner experience of your sexual orientation will fluctuate; it usually stays constant for most men.

As you think about your goals throughout this book, concentrate on your wants, your inner experiences—not your fears. Watch out for the "shoulds" that come from society, traditional morality, family, and so forth. Lest you drive yourself crazy trying to figure out what others want for you, remember that no one but you gets to live your life. As you read this book and work through the exercises, remember that your sexual orientation has qualities that are unique to who you are, just as your physical makeup and personality characteristics are unique to who you are.

his sexuality. He also began to practice the violin again and reconnected with a male friend he'd met through work years before.

One aspect of coming out, then, is being true to yourself about your sexuality. This is important to your whole psychological well-being. And yet, in some situations you may find that your sexual orientation has little to do with who you are.

To help realize and emphasize the importance of including your sexuality in your whole person, answer the following questions:

Do you think you'd be an entirely different person if your sexual orientation was different? How?

_____

_____

_____

_____

Identify a time or situation when you revealed your sexual orientation to a particular person and it enriched your sense of self.

_____

_____

_____

_____

How did this experience feel?

_____

_____

_____

_____

How would you be different if you had *not* come out at that time, or in that situation, to that person?

_____

_____

_____

_____

Stretching Your "Comfort Zone"

Paying attention to your sexual orientation as it fits into your evolving self is a significant step to defining who you are. But you must also be willing to take some risks and let go of the comfort that interferes with being true to your self. You may be stuck in a place that feels safe right now, but in the long run is only doing you harm by preventing change and growth.

Many GBQ men in therapy are exploring potential areas of personal growth. These areas may seem like dark waters, and these men are wary of wading into them. Stretching your comfort zones, however, is how you grow and enrich your life. If you take healthy risks, you'll evolve and find your best and creative capabilities as a GBQ man.

Let's identify some areas where you want to take risks to clarify your sexual orientation and be true to yourself. Coming out to parents, one of the most difficult processes of an evolving sexual orientation, is one example. Another is letting your natural body language show. Another less measurable risk might be accepting and freeing the diverse aspects of your real self, without worrying about what they reveal of you to others. Going through these possibly anxiety-provoking processes can create profound positive changes in your psychological health, improve your self-image, give you freedom from secrecy, and so forth.

Use the chart below to indicate what specifically you want to change about your identity and behavior as a GBQ man at this time in your life. List the change areas, the potential benefit this "risk" will have on your current life, and what you think is needed to begin the change process. When you fill in the middle column, estimate the degree to which the risk will help you be truer to your internal self and your sexual identity, and ultimately how it will improve your feelings about yourself as a whole person. Use the following descriptions to determine how a particular risk may benefit you in stretching your comfort zones: No Change, Mild, Moderate, Significant, or Profound. An example is provided.

Specific Area	Potential Benefit	What I Need to Do to Begin
Tell my sister that my "roommate" is really my lover	*Moderate*	*Call her next weekend*
Stop trying to convince myself that I'm interested in women as more than friends	*Significant*	*Break my date with Susan*
_____	_____	_____
_____		_____
_____		_____
_____	_____	_____
_____		_____
_____		_____
_____	_____	_____
_____		_____
_____		_____
_____	_____	_____
_____		_____
_____		_____
_____	_____	_____
_____		_____
_____		_____
_____	_____	_____
_____		_____

Identifying the areas in which you want to take risks and grow is only the beginning of your journey. At some point, you will have to decide to actually take the risk or not. Ultimately, these decisions are up to you, but as you read on, your path will become more clear.

3

Getting Out of Your Own Way

[N]or is coming out at the age of fourteen the same as coming out at forty-five, though the adolescent may be looking toward a long future and the man at mid-life may be reconciling time passed with an awareness of a limited future. Both generations face a similar psychological trajectory composed of necessary developmental crises that must be mastered to achieve a positive gay identity and life of integrity and satisfaction.

—S. Seigal and E. Lowe,
Uncharted Lives

Stretching beyond your comfort zone requires you to take a good look at yourself, your behaviors, and your emotions. Right now, deep-seated beliefs and suppressed emotions may be acting as defenses, preventing you from evolving and embracing your true identity. In this chapter, you'll learn about these defensive styles—where they come from, how they become obstacles to future growth, and how to work on changing them.

There are many ways of looking at *defenses*. Modern psychology more or less defines defenses (and coping) as emotional, cognitive, and behavioral ways people employ to protect themselves against real or imagined threat. Sometimes having same-sex feelings is experienced as a threat, due to outside criticisms and reactions. Eventually, though, these negative messages may start to come from yourself (through self-talk, thoughts, and feelings) and can develop into a well-worn pattern of defensive behavior. These behaviors can leave you stuck in evolutionary limbo—satisfied with just "getting by" in life. Your goal should be to enhance your identity and move forward with a healthy sense of yourself as a GBQ man.

As you read this section, try to distinguish which of your defenses you're conscious of and which ones you're not. Also try to determine which of your defenses are the result of real threats versus imagined ones. Keep in mind that your defenses may have helped you to survive in your family of origin, in school, with authority figures, and with friends. Defenses such as the ones discussed here may have served to protect you from being humiliated, made fun of, emotionally hurt, physically abused, or harassed. Usually these defenses cease to be useful to you as you mature. They may have become habits, however, and habits are hard to outgrow.

The following paragraphs discuss defensive feelings, thoughts, and behaviors that may prevent you from learning about a healthier, more proactive approach to coming out—to yourself and to others.

Fear

As a therapist, I've found that the feeling most frequently blocking the way to personal growth is fear. GBQ men who are struggling with fear learned at an early age to hide, avoid, withdraw, become invisible, or even strike back. As adults, however, they are capable of identifying other options for themselves to make sure they are safe. But memories of past incidents often interfere with the ability to be who they are as sexual beings and embrace other, more positive options.

I know firsthand the emotional and physical fear that happens when an angry person screams "Faggot!" out the car window, shaking a fist at me as I walk with a friend down the street. Of course, your own fears may be the same or different from mine, may be conscious or unconscious, may be of past, present, or future events.

One of the most common fears a GBQ man must face is that his sexual orientation will result in put-downs, snubs, or even rejection from friends or family members. When Rick finally shared his feelings for men with his best friend, Martin, he was confronted with anger and shock. Martin told Rick that his lifestyle was not something he could agree with and he did not want to be associated with Rick anymore. You may be afraid something like this will happen to you.

In examining your fears, start with specific instances that have struck fear in you as a gay, bisexual, or questioning man. List some situations that still bring up fear when you think of them, and your age when each situation occurred.

Age   Situation or Event

_____   _____
                   _____
                   _____
_____   _____
                   _____
                   _____
                   _____
_____   _____
                   _____
                   _____
                   _____
_____   _____
                   _____
                   _____
                   _____
_____   _____
                   _____
                   _____

Which of the above instances continue to frighten you?

_____
_____
_____

Briefly, describe how these fears currently limit you.

_____
_____
_____

How do you want to change the way these fears continue to influence you?

_____
_____
_____

Now add to your understanding about your own specific fears by reading the following list of common fears for GBQ men coming out about their sexual orientation. Check the ones that are true for you now.

I am afraid that

_____ Others—friends, employees, family—won't want to be associated with me

_____ People will call me names and verbally abuse me

_____ I will be physically harmed

_____ People will judge my sexual interests instead of getting to know me as a whole person

_____ Others will think that I have been sexually abused in my past

_____ I will be judged based on negative stereotypes

_____ Others will think I molest children or am attracted to young boys

_____ My parents and family will reject me and will not want to be around me

_____ My parents, friends, and family won't love me anymore

_____ My parents, friends, and family will put me down or snub me

_____ Friends will abandon me

_____ I won't be able to get a job, will lose my job, or won't be promoted

_____ I will be perceived as "less of a man" or "unmanly"

_____ Others will think I am strange, weird, sick, or perverted

_____ I will become promiscuous

_____ I will contract HIV

_____ Heterosexual men will think I want sex with them and won't want to be friends

_____ I will become an alcoholic

_____ I am doomed to a life of depression and loneliness

_____ Men will not be interested in me sexually

_____ Other men will only be interested in sex, not in having an intimate relationship

_____ I will "stick out" and people will notice me

_____ I will become an anonymous member of "the gay community" and lose my individuality

_____ (other) _____

_____ (other) _____

_____ (other) _____

And on the lighter side . . .

_____ I will shop 'til I drop

_____ I will watch every Judy Garland movie

_____ My house will always be immaculate

_____ I will be compelled to collect all the Barbra Streisand CDs

_____ I will spend an enormous amount of time making gourmet meals and gardening

In the course of this exercise, you may have learned that most of your fears are just that: fears. They are not reality. For example, while it's true that friends and family members are often surprised to find out you are gay or bisexual, many also realize that you are still the same person you were before you came out to them. Occasionally, your fears can help you stay safe in a potentially hurtful situation, such as when you're considering coming out to a fellow employee who may be gossipy or bigoted.

Nevertheless, pat yourself on the back at this point, because you can now recognize your potential fears. The next time you find yourself paralyzed or limited by fear, make a decision to ask yourself these questions:

- How likely is this to happen to me?

- What consequences am I really afraid of?

- What will really happen if I avoid or confront this person or situation? What will I miss out on?

- What, if anything, do I want to do about this fear or situation?

Then move forward. Go *beyond* your comfort zones. If you can identify that your fear is irrational, you can move beyond it.

Anger

Anger is frequently just on the other side of fear and you may not know how to express it. Anger may have been used in hurtful ways against you. You may have learned to split it off or avoid it, to keep from becoming like the aggressors in your life. Over time, anger can damage your view of yourself and keep you from obtaining what you want in life. But assertive forms of expression are in fact *desirable alternatives* to hurtful aggression. They are direct, clear, and they promote a positive sense of self. Standing up for yourself keeps you strong.

The following are indirect expressions of anger and can be destructive to love and communication. Of course, a little bit of these once in a while is only human, but their cumulative effects are hurtful to you and others. Identify the ones that are common for you. Then decide which ones you want to start to change. Write an example that fits for you and explain what you want to do differently.

Sarcasm

Around groups of friends and acquaintances, Randy is often caustic. He thinks it's a way to be funny, but he realizes he is really expressing hostility for not being accepted by his peers and for feeling alienated as a teenager.

My own example:

_____

_____

_____

_____

A more direct approach:

_____

_____

_____

_____

Putting Others Down

Joe often makes fun of other people and their shortcomings to divert the focus from his internalized self-hate.

My own example:

_____

_____

_____

_____

A more direct approach:

_____

_____

_____

_____

Pushing Others Away

Kurt nearly always sabotages potential long-term relationships by getting angry over relatively minor concerns.

My own example:

_____

_____

_____

_____

A more direct approach:

_____

_____

_____

_____

Self-Pity

George is always whining, "They're all prejudiced because I'm homo-sexual!"

My own example:

_____

_____

_____

_____

A more direct approach:

_____

_____

_____

_____

Moodiness

Bob acts mopey, sad, and depressed whenever he's with his family. He realizes he's really angry because his family rejected his male lover.

My own example:

_____

_____

_____

_____

A more direct approach:

_____

_____

_____

_____

Avoiding Responsibility

Adrian often fails to follow through with promises or plans made with his friends. When they attempt to confront him about this, he treats them with disdain.

My own example:

_____

_____

_____

A more direct approach:

_____

_____

_____

_____

Self-Loathing and Self-Destruction

Carl carefully avoids expressing his anger at his parents' religious judgments of him. He frequents bars, drinking too much and looking for men who'll accept him and have sex with him.

My own example:

_____

_____

_____

_____

A more direct approach:

_____

_____

_____

_____

Other

My own example:

_____

_____

_____

_____

A more direct approach:

_____

_____

_____

_____

Shoulds and Expectations

Shoulds are thought processes that tell you you have to fit into a particular mold or label—for instance, "I should be interested in women sexually." These should-thoughts may be conscious, but the older you are, the more likely it is they've become automatic responses. Therefore, rediscovering your shoulds is critical to ending their interference with the growth of your unique, creative self.

Expectations are thought processes that can predetermine a situation's outcome by contributing to anticipatory feelings and thoughts that contaminate your view of reality (that is, your view of yourself as well as the world around you). Like shoulds, expectations can be unconscious and automatic because they may have been planted deep in your belief system during childhood. Excessive fearful expectations can get in the way of being spontaneous, honest in your interactions, at ease with yourself, and capable of handling life's little hassles.

For example, Sean always expected others to surpass him in love and artistic endeavors. In therapy he recognized that his parents had consistently put his older brother first in their priorities, inadvertently teaching him that he was supposed to wait and not make waves. Once Sean uncovered the root of his expectations, he felt empowered and began to try out some new behaviors. He actively pursued various art venues with his work. He started dating men and women in whom he was interested, rather than waiting for his friends to pass him the "leftovers."

Destructive Behavioral Patterns

Various types of unhealthy behavioral patterns may show up among GBQ men. These behavior patterns may be outward examples of long-standing negative beliefs and feelings about yourself. The way you act may reflect your fears, shoulds, expectations, and the shame you feel. (We'll look at shame in chapter 4.)

As you continue working through this chapter, keep in mind that your goal is to recognize how you stifle being true to yourself and meeting your own needs and to develop alternatives that help you love, learn, and contribute to the world as a gay or bisexual man. If you find yourself feeling too negative or uncomfortable while reading about all of these self-defeating thoughts and behaviors, take a break before continuing on with the material. Above all, be patient with yourself and look to these sections as sources of possible positive change.

The following list includes a few of the unhealthy patterns common to men struggling with shame and accepting their sexual orientation. Scan the list and check off all the things you do to yourself that are bad for you in one way or another. This exercise will be most helpful if you are honest. You will be able to explore how you want to change any of these behaviors later in this chapter.

As you work, be aware of how you are currently manifesting these patterns—in what behavior and to what extent. If you think you fall into the "severe" range (that is, if the behavior occurs frequently) or in the "serious" range (that is, you sometimes have suicidal feelings), or if you have many of these behaviors to some extent, you may want to seek professional help.

_____ I drink too much alcohol

_____ I abuse drugs (prescription or illicit)

_____ I eat too much

_____ I starve myself (anorexia or bulimia)

_____ I socialize only with particular groups, such as "pretty" people, gay men, or wealthy individuals

_____ I avoid other people in general

_____ I stay away from challenging situations

_____ I am excessively oversensitive or "delicate"

_____ I am superficial and flighty

_____ I am a perfectionist—compulsive about myself, my home, my work

_____ I am overattentive to physical appearance

_____ I am overattentive to issues of health or illness

_____ I am unreliable

_____ I have aversion, hatred, or prejudice toward certain groups, such as women or heterosexuals

_____ I don't take responsibility for my own behavior

_____ I am selfish or have an inflated sense of my importance (a "holier than thou" stance)

_____ I regularly rebel against authority figures

_____ I verbally abuse others

_____ I allow others to verbally abuse me

_____ I physically abuse others

_____ I allow others to physically abuse me

_____ I have unsafe sex

_____ I have sex in dangerous situations

_____ I have sex with a lot of people I don't know

_____ I let others make decisions for me

_____ I don't exercise or physically exert myself

_____ I cut myself or self-mutilate

_____ I have tried to kill myself

_____ _____

_____ _____

_____ _____

_____ _____

Personality Stalemates

Everybody gets stuck sometimes in certain patterns. You have an opportunity here to identify the personality patterns that inhibit you from being able to be authentic, take good care of yourself, meet your needs, and realize your potential in love, work, or play. While patterns may occur to one degree or another with GBQ men, these personality stalemates exist regardless of sexual orientation. A few of these patterns and stereotyped personalities are

- The curmudgeon (he puts everybody and everything down— nothing's ever right or good enough)

- The "old lady" (he gossips, takes few risks, complains, focuses on what's not right, stays at home, seems fragile and cautious)

- The perfectionist

- The deferential/passive man

- The prince (he expects to be catered to, feels entitled, considers himself "better than" or "special," is self-centered, uses material objects to promote his uniqueness)

- The in-your-face activist

- The peacemaker

Take a moment to see if any of the above apply to you. Maybe you have another personality style that gets you "stuck." Write down the patterns that interfere with being authentic and meeting your goals as a GBQ man.

_____

_____

_____

_____

Now be proactive: Write down some ways you can rework or fine-tune yourself, making positive changes in your personality stalemate. Some examples: seeking out a self-help group; finishing this book; keeping a journal; committing to six months of therapy.

_____

_____

_____

_____

The Peacemaker: The Guy Everybody Likes

The peacemaker is one of the most common personality patterns that interferes with the healthy development of a positive sexual orientation. Even if you don't think this pattern is relevant to you, I recommend you read through this section anyway. If you're sure it doesn't apply to you, you can then skip the exercise and move on.

Putting yourself second to others out of desire to be liked others is the main characteristic of the peacemaker. This behavior can have multiple origins, but adopting the role of peacemaker may spring from ignoring yourself, your wants, and your needs. It can be caused by fear or shame about your sexual orientation.

Being the peacemaker is a common pattern for individuals who have felt "different" or sensitive in some way. Perhaps you've been ostracized because of your particular interests, your race or ethnicity, or because you don't excel at sports or other activities deemed "appropriate" by family and friends. Maybe you've felt isolated because you've had gay feelings and no one to talk to about them. You may have been in a caregiver or peacemaker role because you were the first born in your family or had to care for a parent who was alcoholic, ill, or disabled. Perhaps you've lived with parents who are overworked or irresponsible. For one reason or another, you have learned to please others before you please yourself.

GBQ men often feel compelled to work hard or avoid making waves in order to be liked because they fear discrimination, feel different from everyone else, and expect abandonment if they reveal their real selves.

A wise friend once said to me, "You know, the older you get, the less you care what other people think of you." While this is often true, your need to be liked by others and to keep the peace also depends on your level of self-confidence and self-acceptance of the various aspects of your identity. And as a GBQ man, this must include learning to be comfortable with your sexual orientation.

Take a minute now to think about how much the following factors influence your decisions about your actions and your conversations with others. Rate the items from 0 to 10, with 0 indicating no influence at all and 10 indicating that the issue affects you in almost every way. Then, for each of the questions, think of a situation or relationship in which you would like to change the pattern of behavior.

How important is it to you that others like you? _____
What would you like to change about this need? (Name a specific situation and/or person.)

_____

_____

_____

_____

To what degree did you play peacemaker when you were growing up in your family of origin? _____ What would you like to change about this behavior? (Name a specific situation and/or person.)

_____

_____

_____

_____

To what degree do you currently try to play peacemaker with friends? _____ What would you like to change about this behavior? (Name a specific situation and/or person.)

_____

_____

_____

_____

Are you a peacemaker at work? _____ What would you like to change about this behavior? (Name a specific situation and/or person.)

_____

_____

_____

_____

Are you a peacemaker with family? _____ What would you like to change about this behavior? (Name a specific situation and/or person.)

_____

_____

_____

_____

Are you a peacemaker with acquaintances or lovers? _____
What would you like to change about this behavior? (Name a specific situation and/or person.)

_____

_____

_____

_____

Creating Your Path to Positive Evolution

Because the shoulds and expectations in life, as well as your own negative thoughts, limit you in such a subtle manner, you may not realize how much power you have in working to create your own future. If you continue working on defining your evolving self, you will have a much clearer appreciation for where you are now and where you want to be in your developing life cycle and structure. Not to mention that you may feel better about yourself knowing that you are not alone and that many other GBQ men have had to create their own identities and communities from scratch. Take a moment to think about decisions you have made in the various areas of your life—home, family, friends, and work. Consider your decisions about what you share and how you act in relation to your sexual orientation. Were you influenced by fear, by should-thoughts, by others' expectations of you, by wanting to be liked? Is this how you want to live? The only way to break free of these obstacles is by challenging them.

Overcoming Fear and Anger

Fear and anger are obstacles that you can *choose* to eliminate. By understanding these and other obstacles to emotional growth, you are on the road to feeling better about yourself and getting more comfortable with who you are.

Of course, your anger can also be helpful. It may motivate you to speak up for yourself, avert hurtful behaviors by others, and create positive changes. Jay, for example, used to believe his anger would come out in explosive or inappropriate ways, so he put on a smiling face and avoided anger at all costs. As he learned to approach his anger in healthier ways, he began to speak up when others made jokes about gay people. He talked about his rage against social and political discrimination. Eventually, Jay turned his anger into positive activism; he joined a local task force to fight discrimination against gays and lesbians and create opportunities for gay teens in the local high schools.

As a GBQ man, your anger may also be frightening for you. But if you can take control of it, your anger can propel you to be an advocate for your personal pride.

Shedding the Shoulds

Try the following exercise as a way to shed the negative shoulds of your sexual orientation and clarify your personal meaning of what is right for you.

First, see if you can identify a *positive* should, purpose, or meaning for your sexuality. For example, many of my clients work to develop a conviction that they are gay or bisexual because it is a core aspect of their sexual desires *as well as* their love identity. They should be true to themselves. Other men decide that challenging bigotry and discrimination is an important purpose in their life, and that their sexuality is an extension of their contribution to peace in our world.

Complete this statement:

Being a gay or bisexual man provides a purpose or meaning in my life because

_____

_____

_____

_____

Second, make the following commitments to yourself and your sexual orientation:

- Stop thinking about what's *wrong* with you, about what you *should* be doing, and what others *expect* of you.

- Start thinking about what's *right* with you, about your strengths, and what you want to be doing that is consistent with your values.

- Create a *loyalty* to being who you are in all facets of your life, including your relationships, work, hobbies, passions, and future goals.

Third, write down or tell someone close to you about your commitment to live true to your sexual orientation as it now stands for you.

_____

_____

_____

_____

Future Making

Do this fate-changing exercise, which has been adapted from Tony Robbins' destiny exercise, to create a sense of control over your future.

Choose a quiet place and let yourself relax. Pick one of the behavioral obstacles or peacemaking situations you've identified as one you'd like to change, then put it in terms of how you want to be, what you want to share, or how you want to act. For example, Keith was a self-proclaimed "people pleaser," constantly putting aside his own needs for the good of others. He wanted to change his behavior by taking better care of himself. Since he was afraid that he would be perceived as selfish, he specified in his response to this exercise that he wanted to find a happy medium between people-pleasing and selfishness. He wrote down a few specific situations including "not making waves at work by asking for a raise," and "not upsetting my family by telling them I'm bisexual and involved with a man."

What behavior(s) do you want to change?

_____

_____

_____

_____

Now imagine leaving the chosen behavior or situation unchanged. Imagine yourself each step of the way, with everything as it is now: six months, one year, five years, ten years, and twenty years down the road. How will you think, feel, or act? Where will you be and with whom? Where will you be financially? With friends and family? In other words, what will your life be like if you don't change your actions? Make some notes here about what you imagine.

_____

_____

_____

_____

Next, see yourself *changing* some aspect of how you act. Again, imagine yourself each step of the way: six months, one year, five years, ten years, and twenty years down the road. With the situation changed, how will you think, feel, or act? Where will you be and with whom? Where will you be financially? With friends and family? How will you and your life be different if you change that one aspect of your behavior?

_____

_____

_____

_____

Finally, compare the two scenes. Look at how, by altering only one aspect of your life, you can significantly transform your future. Keith imagined what it would be like if he continued going to work without asking for a raise he knew he deserved. He saw himself becoming more frustrated and resentful. Then he visualized himself mustering up the courage to walk into his supervisor's office and calmly ask for a raise. He knew it would be difficult for him to do, but when comparing the two possible outcomes, he decided it was worth the risk.

Which of your scenes do you prefer and why?

_____

_____

_____

_____

If you haven't yet included sexual orientation in this exercise, do it now. Consider changing an aspect of your approach to sexual orientation—such as coming out to someone you love. What would happen? Would it create profound positive changes in your self-esteem and other specific areas of your life?

_____

_____

_____

_____

Keith visualized how different it would be to be able to introduce his lover to his family and share family activities with his lover. After accepting the fact that it would make his parents uncomfortable, Keith decided that, in the long run, being open with his family would be better for everyone involved. He hoped that by decreasing the shame, fear, and dishonesty in his life, he would create potentially more intimate relationships. And it did indeed. Though it was difficult for him to share this information, it eventually opened a whole new arena for positive exchanges with his parents and his brothers. He began to participate more fully in the family gatherings along with his lover, and forever changed his future to one of increased hope and intimacy.

Making a Change

Creating and structuring your own life cycle by paying attention to your evolving identity and life structure has some very real benefits. It gives you the freedom to determine what is right for your individual circumstances and needs. You'll be able to reinforce for yourself that you aren't required to fit into a particular gay or bisexual model. Continue to pay attention to the fact that *evolving* means having the freedom to grow and change. Be patient with yourself if you find you aren't able to figure out quickly how you feel or what you want for yourself. Don't compare yourself to others or allow shoulds and expectations to corner you. And give yourself a lot of positive reinforcement for facing the tasks of coming out and going against the grain.

Creating your personal developmental life cycle and life structure may be a difficult process. Sometimes it takes a lot of work to shape what is right for you. It's somewhat like being told to bake a cake without a recipe or build a cabinet without a drawing. Knowledge of how to get the ingredients or the parts, knowledge of what they taste or look like doesn't tell you exactly what goes into the finished product. Without a plan you don't know for sure how long to cook your batter or how to fit together your wood. Needless to say, the cake may taste awful and the cabinet may be tilted—but at least you tried. That's why there are books like this one—to provide you with some recipes and strategies.

If you stay stuck in heterosexual definitions of yourself—or even gay/bisexual definitions, for that matter—you may wake up one day and find that you've ignored the evolving aspects of your sexuality, tastes, and interests. Being a GBQ man pushes you to acknowledge the freedom you have and to continually explore your personal changes.

Take some time to notice what has already changed for you in your life. In the following exercise, I've suggested some categories and time periods for you to consider in terms of your GBQ self; use them to describe what has changed for you. (These are suggested categories and intervals; you may not need to use all of them.)

Since I started reading this book, the following things have changed for me:

- Beliefs/Thoughts: (Example: As a bisexual person, I now feel worthy of respect from gay and heterosexual people.)

_____

_____

_____

- Feelings: (Example: I'm excited about being more open about my sexual orientation.)

_____

_____

_____

- Behaviors: (Example: I've stopped using alcohol to make meeting men easier.)

_____

_____

_____

- Desires: (Example: I want to have a partner I can be sexual and intimate with and who understands my feelings.)

_____

_____

_____

- Goals: (Example: I want to be more aware of how other people's opinions limit my behavior.)

_____

_____

_____

In the last year, the following things have changed for me:

- Beliefs/Thoughts:

_____

_____

_____

- Feelings:

_____

_____

_____

- Behaviors:

_____

_____

_____

- Desires:

_____

_____

_____

- Goals:

_____

_____

_____

In the last five years, the following things have changed for me:

- Beliefs/Thoughts:

_____

_____

_____

- Feelings:

_____

_____

_____

- Behaviors:

_____

_____

_____

- Desires:

  _____

  _____

  _____

- Goals:

  _____

  _____

  _____

In the last _____ days/months/years, the following things have changed for me:

- Beliefs/Thoughts:

  _____

  _____

  _____

- Feelings:

  _____

  _____

  _____

- Behaviors:

  _____

  _____

  _____

- Desires:

  _____

  _____

  _____

- Goals:

  _____

  _____

  _____

Since I first realized I have gay or bisexual feelings, the following things have changed for me:

- Beliefs/Thoughts:

_____

_____

_____

- Feelings:

_____

_____

_____

- Behaviors:

_____

_____

_____

- Desires:

_____

_____

_____

- Goals:

_____

_____

_____

In the future, I imagine the following things will change in or evolve from my GBQ self:

- Beliefs/Thoughts:

_____

_____

_____

- Feelings:

_____

_____

- Behaviors:

- Desires:

- Goals:

Remain open to what emerges from your thoughts, feelings, dreams, and passions. Consider what develops: Is it a part of your next developmental stage as a GBQ man, or is it just a flash in the pan? You may have explored some new recipes and looked at a few blueprints; maybe you've created a few grease fires in the kitchen or banged your thumb with the hammer. Remember, it's all part of the process.

Suggestions to Support Your Evolving GBQ Self

While you're evolving, you may settle into some comfortable, stable ways of being a GBQ man in your world—ways that are just right for you. That's good, too. For example, you may settle down with a partner. You may start to feel more solid in your sexuality as a gay or bisexual man. Your evolution will still continue in other areas. Here are a few pointers to keep in mind as you move through your particular developmental life cycle:

Be Unique

Focus on letting your uniqueness shine through. Find opportunities to share your personal thoughts and feelings. Express yourself through your clothing, ethnicity, language, interests, or behavior. For example, Joseph started to look for and buy clothes that matched his personality, instead of trying to appear "straight."

Avoid being a rebel just to be different, though—it usually turns people off, and they don't get the opportunity to see you for your true, special qualities.

Don't Be Afraid to Make Mistakes

People learn more from mistakes than successes. Experiment; be bold enough to try on some new ways of being or expressing who you are. Besides, it helps you to accept your humanity, and most people want to be around others who are human, not perfect. If you really do "blow it," you can always apologize and rethink your actions. Remember what you have learned, and rehearse mentally before doing it the next time. For example, at a party, Lance met a man he found interesting. When Lance asked him if he was gay, the man frowned and walked away. Lance found out what he wanted to know, but decided he would try another approach next time.

Be Responsible

Think about what you want before jumping in head first—there may not be any water in the pool. Treat your body and your soul like the precious things they are, to be honored and cared for. Be safe with sex. Take responsibility for your actions. Apologize if you have hurt someone's feelings. And remember to treat yourself the same way you would treat a best friend. For example, Alex tended to treat people as if they were objects for his love, sex, and emotional fulfillment. So, he set a goal to be more thoughtful in his relationships with others and to ask them about their feelings and needs.

Be Three-Dimensional

Work on developing a range of interests or focus on the things you are good at. Create feeling labels and a vocabulary for your facial and body expressions so you can better identify and enrich your inner experiences and reactions. Cultivate diverse friendships and deep, caring relationships. Find a sense of purpose in your day-to-day life and actions that has meaning to you; nurture your creative, adventurous, even wild, sides through expressive arts, or through the use of your body in sports or movement. Think the unthinkable about who you are and what you want out of life, love, and work; then let your mind expand into the possibilities. Shed fear, unless it serves a direct survival purpose.

For example, Wayne had always kept pretty much to himself and had few interests outside of work, a few gay friends, and Madonna's latest recording. He decided to enroll in a meditation and yoga class, began keeping a journal of his feelings, dreams, and fantasies, and started taking weekend hikes with acquaintances from the local ecology group.

Now that you're at the end of this chapter, reflect back on what has happened as you worked through the exercises. Are you allowing yourself to grow and change? Do you know what's preventing you from being true to yourself and your sexual orientation? Have your feelings about yourself changed? Notice how your awareness of defense mechanisms has improved your ability to identify and challenge your own obstacles. And pay particular attention to the power you have to alter unhealthy patterns and create beneficial changes in your emotions, thoughts, and behavior. Indeed, you can be your own champion for a positive sexual orientation and an evolving self, no matter what your obstacles.

4

Healing a Lifetime of Shame and Guilt

Shame fuels hatred towards ourselves, just as it fuels hatred towards others. Shame is the affect from which all stigmas and taboos spring.

—G. Kaufman and L. Raphael,
Coming Out of Shame

Now that you've explored your identity and personal obstacles in more depth, you're in a better position to handle additional obstacles to cultivating your positive sense of identity as a GBQ man. In this chapter, you'll examine the other major limitations to your sense of personal pride: shame and guilt. The focus will be not only on identifying your shame and guilt, but also on continuing to emphasize solutions for manifesting your positive sexual orientation.

Shame versus Guilt

Although they may feel similar, there is a difference between shame and guilt. The simplest distinction is that guilt is about what you do, and shame is about who you are. The following statements comparing guilt and shame are from John Grace (1992). My own modifications are shown in brackets.

Guilt [can tell me] I made a mistake.
Shame says I am a mistake.

Guilt [may ask] what is to be done?
Shame says nothing can be done.

With guilt, reparation may be made.
With shame, the damage seems beyond repair.

Guilt [can] energize.
Shame paralyzes.

Guilt [may] motivate us to improve or accept ourselves and the world.
Shame intimidates us to destroy and reject ourselves and the world.

Guilt can reveal the truth.
Shame always lies.

As a GBQ man, you are particularly vulnerable to the effects of both guilt and shame because of your sexual feelings and actions. Your guilt and shame may be perpetuated by the myths springing from your culture, society, and religious upbringing that say engaging in same-sex activities is sinful, promiscuous, depraved, perverted, and selfish. Too often, guilt and shame play off of one another, feeding your negative thoughts and chipping away at your self-esteem.

As a young man, you may have internalized negative beliefs and messages from peers, parents, church, the media, and so on. No doubt you receive plenty of reinforcement from the heterosexual point of view about how you should feel, think, and act. As a result, by the time you reach young adulthood, you come to believe that your own perceptions of love and sex are "different" from mainstream society's and therefore wrong. You learn to mistrust your basic needs, feelings, and motivations.

Experiencing shame and self-mistrust can create substantial lags in development of self-identity and sexual orientation. It can erode your self-confidence. You may adopt defense mechanisms such as those discussed in chapter 3—guilt and shame frequently lie behind such defense mechanisms. But, if you take the time now to identify the source of and replace destructive forms of guilt and shame, you can circumvent much of your pain and discomfort about sexual orientation.

One of the most prominent sources of guilt and shame for GBQ men is organized religion and the moral judgments it passes. For example, leaders of the Catholic Church and certain other denominations have made pronouncements that reinforce guilt and shame for men who love men. Many of these institutions have announced that they embrace all people, all members of their congregation, including homosexuals—as long as they don't act on their feelings. Because of such judgments, you may feel forced to split off the loving and sexual part of yourself. In the end, what you feel is shame about your true identity and guilt about your need for same-sex intimacy.

Luis, age twenty-three, was raised a strict Catholic. Both his father and priest had taught him "real men" can't love other men. His priest had said that homosexuality has a weakness of spirit and homosexual people went to hell. When he moved to the United States from Mexico, he married a woman and hid his same-sex feelings, convinced he was one of a few condemned homosexuals. He developed a deep sense of guilt and shame and engaged in compulsive prayer rituals that interfered with his ability to focus on his work. Unfortunately, Luis also engaged in anonymous, unsafe sexual encounters in public places. He found an accepting group, Gay Catholic Dignity, and over time began to see the destructive nature of his shame and guilt. He then came out to his wife and developed friendships with men and women who would not judge him.

Regardless of age, religion, culture, or family upbringing, everyone is touched by guilt and shame about gay or bisexual feelings. Take a few moments now to identify your specific experiences in these areas.

What Makes You Feel Guilty?

Write out one or more incidents involving same-sex thoughts, feelings, and/or activities that bring up feelings of guilt for you.

_____

_____

_____

_____

How does your guilt lead you to have certain beliefs or act in certain ways with regard to your sexual orientation?

_____

_____

_____

_____

In what ways does guilt about your sexuality limit you?

_____

_____

_____

_____

What Makes You Feel Ashamed?

Write out one or more incidents involving same-sex thoughts, feelings, and/or activities that bring up feelings of shame about who you are.

_____

_____

_____

_____

How does your shame lead you to have certain beliefs or act in certain ways with regard to your sexual orientation?

_____

_____

_____

_____

In what ways does shame about who you are sexually limit you?

_____

_____

_____

_____

Unconscious Guilt and Shame

In the previous exercise, you may have been able to think of examples of guilt and shame easily—or maybe you couldn't come up with any at all. If you didn't, it may be that you have little guilt or shame about your sexuality. Or it may be that you've buried your guilt and shame so deep, even you are unaware of them.

Unconscious guilt and shame often play the role of silent soul-killers. While you've probably worked hard to ignore these feelings, your sense of personal pride as a GBQ man is at continued risk if they remain unchecked.

When you are acting out of unconscious guilt or shame, you may

- Feel constantly ambivalent or depressed about your same-sex feelings

- Have mostly anonymous, clandestine, or degrading sexual encounters

- Abuse drugs or alcohol to reduce anxiety in social situations

- Constantly isolate yourself

- Avoid situations that can trigger guilt or shame

These behaviors, as well as the defensive obstacles you identified in chapter 3, can serve as red flags to warn you about your unconscious shame and guilt. Pay attention to these red flags; they are signs that can direct you toward positive possibilities and changes in your life.

Whether you experience conscious or unconscious guilt or shame is not an all-or-nothing issue. You may be able to recognize some of your discomforting emotions but not others. If you were surprised by the kind or number of defensive obstacles that you identified in chapter 3, unconscious guilt and shame may be hard at work in your life. Nevertheless, *awareness* of these patterns can actually jump-start you to make changes in your life.

Don't Be Afraid to Study Your Shame and Guilt

If you feel concerned or overwhelmed by how guilt and shame show up in your life, you'll need to be very patient with yourself. Here are a few strategies to help you deal with your emotions:

- Remind yourself to observe what you don't like about your shame or guilt. Remember that you're "in training" and you have to learn how to treat yourself better, one step at a time.

- If you are feeling overloaded by your emotions or out of control, find a close, safe, positive friend, a therapist, or mentor with whom to talk about your feelings. Talking can help you recognize your patterns.

- Keep a journal. Writing is another way to begin recognizing unconscious guilt and shame. Write about your same-sex feelings and any behaviors that relate to anger and fear, self-blame and hatred. Keeping a journal is a healthy way to release your feelings. You'll also gain some objectivity about the ways you punish yourself and find ways to act differently.

Leave guilt behind for now and focus your energy on understanding and changing shame in your life. Remember: although guilt certainly can immobilize your actions, it may also *stimulate positive change*. Shame, on the other hand, has a more profound negative impact on your identity as a GBQ man.

Sources of Shame in Your Life

You may have already begun to identify your internal sources of shame, from reading the previous discussions and doing the exercises. In this section, you'll have an opportunity to define some external sources from *shame-bound systems*. With regard to sexual orientation, a shame-bound system consists of individuals or groups that perpetuate myths, attitudes, or behaviors that lead GBQ people to feel they are bad or abnormal. Just recognizing these sources and acknowledging their power can sub-stan-tially decrease your self-blame and make it easier to reject those toxic messages and replace them with self-affirming ones.

Identify the sources of negative shame messages you've received about being gay or bisexual by completing the following statements:

My religion/place of worship taught me that being gay or bisexual is

_____

In school, I learned that being gay or bisexual is

_____

My friends and peers talk(ed) about gay or bisexual people as

_____

My parents taught me that being gay or bisexual is

_____

I've read or heard statements in the media that suggest being gay or bisexual is

_____

Now add some of your own statements about other groups or people who have been sources of shame about being gay or bisexual.

_____ taught me that being gay or bisexual is

_____

_____ taught me that being gay or bisexual is

_____

_____ taught me that being gay or bisexual is

_____

Chronicle Your Shame History

I like to refer to specific feelings and incidents of GBQ shame from your past as *peak points*. These incidents may have occurred at home, in school, in church, with friends or peers, at work, and so on. Peak points can trigger feelings of shame and pain even in adulthood. The purpose here is simply to recognize them, so that you can study your reactions—conscious and unconscious.

Nick, a thirty-eight-year-old bisexual man, recalled that at age eight he was seen by his friends kissing another boy. Nick was being affectionate, but his peers began calling him a girl's name, his teacher made him write sentences about how wrong his action was, and his father stopped speaking to him for a week.

Your own example may be less overt than Nick's; maybe your experience was more like Tony's. At age forty-five, Tony remembered how, at fourteen, he used to feel excited when his older brother's handsome friends came to visit. Tony used to follow them around and acted angry and jealous when they didn't include him in their activities. He still feels ashamed and embarrassed when he thinks of how he acted then.

> **Journaling Hint**
>
> When you're journaling, work at further distinguishing between your shame and guilt experiences. When describing your experiences, ask yourself, "Do I fear abandonment by others? Is it because I think I'm unworthy, flawed, or damaged?" That's shame talking. Then ask, "Do I fear punishment? Will I suffer negative consequences for doing something 'wrong'?" That's guilt talking. Your goal here is simply to become more aware of your shame and guilt. This will help you to recognize what you may want to change, so you can begin to actually make those changes—an exercise you'll do later in this chapter.

Keep in mind that identifying your past shame is not about blaming other people. It's about understanding what you have experienced, how it has shaped you, and how to change shame's influence on you.

In the spaces below, indicate the ways you've felt ashamed of yourself as a GBQ man. Try to think of at least one way for each phase of your life. Don't worry, though, if you can come up with only a few examples. It may help you to be very specific in writing an incident down, so have your computer ready or some extra writing paper on hand if you need more space to write.

Early childhood (up to age five):

_____

_____

_____

_____

Childhood (age five to eleven):

_____

_____

_____

_____

Adolescence (age twelve to eighteen):

_____

_____

_____

_____

Early adulthood (age nineteen to twenty-five):

_____

_____

_____

_____

Adulthood (age twenty-six to fifty):

_____

_____

_____

_____

Later adulthood (age fifty-plus):

_____

_____

_____

_____

Hints for Changing Shameful Peak Points

- Take a moment to really *forgive* yourself for what you did not like about what you did.

- Remind yourself to *be compassionate*. Maybe you were only trying to express certain needs, or others did not understand you, or you had limited knowledge—remember that many factors may have been at play.

- Remind yourself that, no matter how painful this was for you, *you managed to survive*. Ask yourself, "How did I get through it? What were my strengths that helped me get through it?"

- Ask yourself, "What could I possibly have changed about the situation, knowing what I knew then?" Keep in mind that while you can't go back and change any of your past shame experiences, you can *change how you deal with them now*. That's what'll help you learn and move ahead.

- Shame feelings tend to be deeply entrenched. If you feel you're still having a tough time undoing shame's influence on you, don't be afraid to *seek outside help*. Recognize when you need the help of a professional, like a psychotherapist. It's the healthy thing to do.

Identify Your Current Shame Patterns

Your present thoughts, feelings, and behavior may still be influenced by your past shame. Same-sex feelings often bring with them a host of rules that gay and bisexual men have learned to live by. Many of these shame-bound rules are established early, at home within families, but the rules also come from schools, friends and peers, religion, and culture.

Following are some typical family rules, identified by Fossum and Mason (1986), that can enforce shame-bound patterns. For each rule, write in examples, feelings, thoughts, or behaviors you experienced specifically as a result of following that rule. Examples are included for each rule.

Control

"Be in control of all feelings, behaviors, and interactions."

Steve has stopped displaying any feelings of affection towards men for fear of being found out as gay. He is controlled, tense, and rigid in the way he holds his body and shows his emotions. He has lost a good deal of spontaneity and has developed a sense of shame about his inability to control his attraction to men.

My example:

_____

_____

_____

Perfection

"If you can't do it right, don't do it at all."

James learned to be "the best little boy in the world" by the age of eight. Unfortunately, he has paid a price for this: He always feels he has to do things perfectly, is unforgiving of others, and has developed into a meticulous housekeeper. James assumes that if he is perfect, no one will look down on him for being attracted to men.

My example:

_____

_____

_____

Blame

"If something doesn't happen as planned, someone must be blamed—yourself or someone/something else."

Joey avoids feeling shame about his gay feelings and about having sex with men by blaming his behavior on alcoholism.

My example:

_____

_____

_____

Denial

"Deny feelings, especially negative or vulnerable ones such as fear, loneliness, need, and same-sex desires."

Joshua has been pretending to be heterosexual for years despite his intense attraction to men. He has a strong sense of shame and as a result forms primarily cold, distant relationships with others.

My example:

_____

_____

_____

Avoidance

"It's better to avoid confrontation or potential rejection."

Morris has a bad habit of rarely being on time. He seldom returns phone calls and often doesn't follow through on commitments to the men he meets. He realizes that his shame about having same-sex feelings has led to a belief that "If I don't really show up, I won't have to experience my anxiety—about my feelings for men and about being 'bad.'"

My example:

_____

_____

_____

Hiding

"Don't talk openly about potentially different, out-of-the-ordinary, disrespectful, shameful, or compulsive behavior."

As a child, Eric once told a friend about his same-sex feelings. His friend laughed and told several other kids in his class, who made fun of him. As an adult, Eric has not told anyone in his family or any of his close friends that he is gay.

My example:

_____

_____

_____

Did you recognize any shame rules you carry with you? If so, you have successfully pinpointed some essential blocks to having personal pride about your sexual orientation. You may want to review the shame-bound rules identified and write new rules that are consistent with your developing sense of positive gay or bisexual beliefs and values.

For example, you could change the control rule, which tells you to "be in control of all feelings, behaviors, and interactions," to say "Be myself, relax, and be comfortable with my natural reactions."

_____

_____

_____

Planning for Shame

A peace above all earthly dignities?
A still and quiet conscience.

—William Shakespeare, *Henry VIII*

Make a Commitment to Change Your Reactions

Society may always have prohibitions and shaming beliefs about sexual behavior. Now that you are more aware of some of your sources of shame, realize that while you may not be able to change them, you can change your *reactions* to them. You can begin this process by making a commitment to yourself to be responsible for your own change and to respond to the world from an internal sense of pride, self-respect, and dignity.

In the next exercise, you'll write down some things you can do to change your reactions to the harmful messages you've identified. Then choose some things you can do to help you feel more self-respect.

For example, Jim is a gay man who wants to alter his reaction to the shame messages he has heard from religious sources. He has decided to attend a Unitarian church and wants to redefine his spirituality in terms of love and acceptance. Jim has made a commitment to improving his self-respect by attending a gay-positive congregation.

Complete these statement(s) about your own commitments:

I will change my old reaction to the _____ shame message by doing the following:

_____

_____

_____

I will change my old reaction to the _____ shame message by doing the following:

_____

_____

_____

I can instill pride about my sexual feelings and identity by doing the following:

_____

_____

_____

I can instill pride about my sexual feelings and identity by doing the following:

_____

_____

_____

Shame happens. You can bet on it. But now you've made a commitment to do something about it. Accept that shame is something you *will* experience at various points in your life. Don't try to pretend you don't feel it. *Avoidance and denial will only force the shame underground.* Avoiding shame can make you even more ashamed—in other words, you may end up being ashamed about your shame. So what can you do that's constructive to overcome everyday shame about your sexuality?

- Accept that shame is a part of your past.

- Be aware of how cultural, family, and ethnic rules may perpetuate shame.

- Recognize your shame triggers.

- Develop alternatives for coping with shame.

If you've done most of the previous exercises, you're already getting better at recognizing what triggers your shame. Continue to identify shame triggers by writing about your same-sex thoughts and feelings and your external sources of shame. Reflect upon past incidents as well as patterns of behavior that may have evolved in response to shame.

This next exercise will help you to actually change your shame reactions. This is one of the most effective methods I have found to help people change automatic thoughts and patterns of behavior.

When you experience shame, take a moment to think about how you would like to change your reaction. Imagine the experience is a videotape. Rewind the experience and "rerecord" a new scene in your head; play it out the way you want it to happen, changing your feelings, reactions, behaviors, or thoughts.

After rerecording your shame incident, you'll be better prepared the next time shame emerges. Realize that you will not do it perfectly the next time, but with practice you'll undoubtedly come closer and closer to your desired result.

Tim rewound his mental videotape of embarrassment and shame that occurred when he met a handsome man at work. He rerecorded the incident, replacing his shame reaction by walking himself through a scene in which he looked the man in the eye and acted as if the man were simply an interesting person. Tim still found the man attractive but did not shy away and turn red (his old reaction). The next time he met an attractive guy, Tim was not nearly as aloof and didn't feel as "weird" (as he called it). He patted himself on the back, realizing the man he met didn't have to have any idea at all about Tim's thoughts or feelings of embarrassment. Tim was now able to be more relaxed with men he found attractive.

Armed with your revamped mental videotapes and the other knowledge of shame you've gathered in this chapter, you are well on your way to developing an increased awareness of shame, coping mechanisms for your shame, and ways of changing your same-sex shame. Let's explore what can take shame's place.

Ultimately, replacing both shame and guilt means allowing your needs and wants, your love for others, and your positive values to take the lead. *You* determine your thoughts, behaviors, and self-image. Instead of being controlled by hurtful past experiences, potentially fearful and threatening current experiences, or worries about what others think of you, your inner world can be determined by positive values, healthy self-talk, self-discipline, and a balance between receiving and contributing to the world around you.

Self-talk is made up of things you tell yourself—thoughts that automatically come to mind and are often based on messages you've received in the past. Negative self-talk usually stems from guilt-inducing and shame-producing messages. It distorts your view of reality and clouds healthy thinking. It can contribute to depression, anger, anxiety, and a myriad of other negative mood states.

To replace shame with assurance and self-esteem and help you form a more solid foundation for pride and personal growth as a GBQ man, you must challenge your negative self-talk and embrace healthy values.

Learn to Use Self-Talk

The following exercise is based on the work of Ronald and Patricia Potter-Efron (1989). It will help you to identify and change common internal shame messages.

Step I

First, work through the following items, noticing whether any of them are true for you. Try to stick to issues of your sexuality. Don't overthink these statements. Ignore the "Who/How" and "New Affirmation" parts for now. Just go through and circle the specific shame reactions that seem most applicable. In the second part of the exercise, you'll fill in the additional information. Ask yourself if these shame messages emerge specifically from your GBQ feelings.

About my same sex feelings, thoughts, and behavior or as a GBQ man, I have the following thoughts:

I am: defective   damaged   broken   a mistake   flawed

Who/how?

New affirmation:

I am: dirty   ugly   unclean   filthy   impure   disgusting
Who/how?

_____

New affirmation:

_____

I am: stupid   dumb   silly   crazy   a jerk
Who/how?

_____

New affirmation:

_____

I am: incompetent   inadequate   useless   inept   incapable   ineffectual
Who/how?

_____

New affirmation:

_____

I am: unlovable   unappreciated   unwanted   not cared for   unworthy
Who/how?

_____

New affirmation:

_____

I am: bad   awful   terrible   evil   horrible   despicable
Who/how?

_____

New affirmation:

_____

I am: pitiful   miserable   insignificant
Who/how?

_____

New affirmation:

_____

I am: *nothing*   *empty*   *worthless*   *invisible*   *irrelevant*

Who/how?

_____

New affirmation:

_____

I deserve: *criticism*   *disapproval*   *condemnation*

Who/how?

_____

New affirmation:

_____

I feel: *ashamed*   *embarrassed*   *humiliated*   *mortified*

Who/how?

_____

New affirmation:

_____

I am: *weak*   *small*   *impotent*   *feeble*   *puny*

Who/how?

_____

New affirmation:

_____

I should not: *be alive*   *exist*   *take up space*

Who/how?

_____

New affirmation:

_____

Step 2

Since you've often learned your shame from specific experiences or other people, go back and fill in the Who/How part. Who provided the message? How did you get the message?

Step 3

Go back and write in, for each shame reaction, a new affirmation to combat the feeling of shame. What you're doing is replacing your shame-inducing self-talk with positive messages.

For example, Zach circled "I am unlovable." He replaced it with "As a bisexual man I deserve love and am a soft, warm person." Dyer circled both "invisible" and "worthless." He replaced it with "I am visible and worthy—I can make myself be seen as a gay man and remind myself I am valuable as a gay man."

Step 4

Lastly, red flag your shame messages in your mind. Each time you catch yourself experiencing your usual reaction to shame messages, replace it with a positive affirmation. This is a powerful tool for changing your automatic thought processes.

Obviously, changing these messages will take more time than what you have invested here. They may be lifelong shame messages that won't disappear the first time you challenge them. Yet, by making a commitment and resolving not to shame yourself and your sexuality, you can rewire the computer in your head and stop these messages from incurring any additional damage. You've been feeding yourself these negative messages for years, so be patient with yourself; take the time to *go beyond shame*.

Develop Healthy Values

Going beyond shame also means being who you are—the unique person you identified in chapter 2. Going beyond shame encourages a sturdier foundation from which to build your self-talk and nourish healthy behavior as a GBQ man.

In their book, *Self-Esteem*, Matt McKay and Patrick Fanning (1993) assert that healthy values are

- *Flexible.* They allow for exceptions and errors to occur (versus being rigid and global).

- *Owned.* They fit into your unique circumstances and identity (versus being automatic thoughts, unquestioned generalizations, or attempts to be liked or accepted by others).

- *Realistic.* They lead to positive consequences for you and others (versus being based on "rightness" or principles set out by other people).

- *Life-enhancing.* They lead you to be nurturing and supportive of yourself and others (versus restricting your life and ignoring your feelings and needs).

Using these definitions, create a healthy value statement about your sexuality. Make sure it allows for you to feel comfortable about your sexual needs and about yourself as GBQ man. For example, Clarke wrote this *owned* value statement about his bisexuality: "I have feelings for both men and women. I desire to date and see whom I want as a long-term partner, based on how I love them instead of how friends or families feel and think."

Make a *flexible* value statement about your same-sex feelings or about yourself as a GBQ man:

_____

_____

_____

Make an *owned* value statement about your same-sex feelings or about yourself as a GBQ man:

_____

_____

_____

Make a *realistic* value statement about your same-sex feelings or about yourself as a GBQ man:

_____

_____

_____

Make a *life-enhancing* value statement about your same-sex feelings or about yourself as a GBQ man:

_____

_____

_____

Now, write a solid self-statement, motto, or mantra that reflects all of your new healthy inner values.

_____

_____

_____

Congratulations! You've done some hard work in this chapter. You have navigated through your shame and are better prepared to deal with it in your future. You have set the stage to nurture yourself through ongoing support and safety.

5

Searching for Safety and Support

Simply stated, a positive affirming community heals the wounds of external oppression.

—John Gonsiorek, *Lesbian, Gay, and
Bisexual Identities Over the Lifespan*

Imagine yourself in a country foreign to you, wandering the streets, lost. You have no money or identification because the knapsack you packed so carefully this morning was stolen by a thief with very quick hands. There are no faces you recognize, no one speaks your language, and you can't read the map because your language dictionary was in the knapsack. It's hot and everything you smell and hear is unfamiliar. Your clothes are different from everyone else's. Even the dog on the street looks strange. You feel yourself getting shaky, then really frightened when you accidentally turn down a dark, seedy alleyway. Suddenly you flash on *home*. Sweet home, with the humdrum of work and laundry and that stack of mail you left unopened. How dearly you would appreciate right now the faces of those who await your return.

While trying to decide whether to strangle your traveling companion for suggesting this "exotic" destination in the first place or to kick yourself for taking the "interesting" way through town, you round the next corner and spy the familiar face of your friend. A moment ago you were cursing him for dragging you to this hellhole, but now he represents something different. You no longer want to render him unconscious or set his eyelashes on fire, because now he's what you need: a haven of safety and—at least temporarily—a familiar, supportive being.

Everyone has taken safety and support for granted. And they didn't have to travel to a foreign country to appreciate what they have. In the last few chapters, you've explored your identity and learned how to work through shame and guilt. Now it's time to take charge and create a sense of safety and support in your world. In this chapter, you will take your own journey into the elusive realm of safety and support, defining for yourself what each of these means to you. You'll see how to recognize the value of safety, how to create and nourish it, and how to identify what you need and want and from whom you want it. Then you'll learn how to go about finding that support—in yourself as well as in others.

Safety and support are critical elements of nurturing. Both are important for protection, solace, growth, and emotional survival. As a GBQ man, you have some unique needs for safety and support. Your sex and love interests may have brought you intense feelings of longing, some scorn or criticism, and admonitions from both internal or external sources. Some or all of this may have left you feeling fearful and lonely.

In order to bask in the joyful moments of being a gay or bisexual man, you need help overcoming the tough times. You need to feel safe from harm's way, emotionally secure, and supported by others in your life.

Setting the Stage

To keep oneself safe does not mean to bury oneself.

—Seneca, "On Peace of Mind," *Moral Essays*

Knowing you are safe and supported is reassuring, it helps you feel worthy, loved, and respected. Even if you have no recognizable support system you can create an inner world that provides a sense of compassion and protection. You can also set goals to put yourself in contact with others who are likely to be there for you emotionally and physically. Many GBQ men have learned to overcome truly outrageous, excruciatingly cruel physical and emotional abuse and abandonment, by discovering unexpected sanctuary in themselves and in others.

Emotional and Physical Safety

What does safety have to do with coming out as a gay or bisexual man? Why is it important to you? Both physical and emotional safety are essential to feeling okay about who you are and free to express your essence to the outside world. Physical safety is a fairly simple concept, defined by feeling protected from bodily harm. For example, you may be worried that a prejudiced person who learns of your sexual orientation may strike out at you in some form of violence. Since the fear and malicious intent some people have towards gays and bisexuals is undeniable, these kinds of worries are not unfounded.

Physical safety is a basic necessity, and it creates a foundation for an ongoing sense of emotional safety. Kyle views safety as knowing that "if someone hassles you or threatens to hurt you, you feel like you have the emotional tools of an aikido black belt, who can handle most anything that confronts him, no matter where he is." Most people never quite acquire the skill of a self-defense master, but you can get to know what you need to keep physically and emotionally safe.

Emotional safety is somewhat more complex to define. In addition to perceptions, thoughts, and feelings that you are free from potential physical harm, it includes feeling protected and free from other people's words, prejudice, verbal abuse, negative attitudes, discrimination, humiliation, shame, defamation of your character, and so forth. Feeling emotionally safe can also result from realizing that others have your best interests at heart.

Ultimately, emotional safety must be defined by you. I can suggest, guide, and borrow from professional and personal experience—but the ultimate source of your definition of safety is your past. Perhaps you recall only vague feelings of safety from your past, but that's a start. Or you may need some assistance from your creative spirit to design a new sense of safety.

Neil, for example, defines safety as a sense of inner comfort; as if "your mind and body have just taken a warm bath and you curl up at home, by the fire and read your favorite novel." On the other hand, Tom describes support as "knowing there are people in my life who I can talk to about the most erotic, weird, or scary thing I can think of and they'll still respect me in the morning." Your goal is to begin providing a place for yourself as a GBQ man to go to—a place in your own soul where you can find or create words, identify people, places, or ideas, to help provide you with improved safety and support, even if it's only for a few moments at a time. In this place, you'll feel secure—about yourself and your environment.

As you work on defining physical and emotional safety for yourself, remember that safety does not mean totally avoiding taking risks. Your sense of safety may come from a particular person or an experience. An example might be receiving a gift from a valued family member or having a conversation with your best buddy.

As a GBQ man, what does physical safety mean to you? (Examples: That I'm not in danger of being hurt by others; that people aren't looking at me in a threatening way.)

_____

_____

_____

_____

What do you need to feel physically safe? (Examples: to be around other people; to know I can physically overpower another person; to know how to think on my feet)

_____

_____

_____

_____

As a GBQ man, what does emotional safety mean to you? (Examples: that I'm not referred to as "weird," "faggot," or "sexually ambivalent"; that my feelings and desires aren't being criticized or judged)

_____

_____

_____

_____

What do you need to feel emotionally safe? (Examples: emotionally supportive people in my life; freedom from criticism or judgment; to know I'm loved or considered special)

_____

_____

_____

_____

You may want to come back to this section and add to your descriptions after you complete the other exercises in this chapter.

Safety-Proofing Your Coming Out

Various threats to your physical and emotional safety can endanger your self-esteem and sense of *psychological safety*. Psychological safety therefore depends on you feeling both physically and emotionally safe. You may want to think about how these two safety mechanisms work together to help you to feel relaxed, free from harm's way, and peaceful. People who experience psychological insecurity may feel flawed and chronically unworthy of love. They may even be paranoid that the world is out to get them or thinks badly of them. Such reactions can lead some people to constantly expect emotional or physical harm.

Clinical experience has demonstrated that GBQ men may be at continued risk of feeling chronically unsafe, fearful of their surroundings, and mistrustful as a result of continued lack of acceptance and blatant discrimination from society. Sometimes your experiences of mistrust and fear may be borne of others' view of you as odd or different. More commonly, however, the state of your hidden self is the villain. If you suspect that everyone who knows or assumes that you are gay or bisexual will ultimately hurt you in some way because of it, you're allowing your hidden self to interpret and convince you of potential threat.

The fact that some GBQ men often feel threatened does not necessarily mean they are clinically paranoid or have a personality disorder. This insecurity may simply be the result of a massive amount of internal or external pressure to try to be something they are not—namely, heterosexual. They may have learned from past experiences to mistrust themselves; or they may have been abused in ways that have left them with unhealed physical and emotional scars.

Feeling a presence or lack of psychological safety can result from past experiences. Answer the following questions to identify threats (real, imagined, or both) and feelings of safety from your past.

Have you ever been made to feel threatened, unsafe, or insecure about being a GBQ man by your family, religion, peers, society in general, or the media? What happened to make you feel that way? Try to think of specific times, people, places, and events. Write down how old you were, where you were living, who was in your life, and so on. Did you feel physically unsafe? Emotionally unsafe? Both?

_____

_____

_____

_____

Have certain *surroundings* or *events* promoted a sense of psychological safety? How? Did they help you express your feelings and opinions? Did they help you feel comfortable and secure?

_____

_____

_____

_____

Did certain *people* promote a sense of psychological safety? How?

_____

_____

_____

_____

Now, turn to your same-sex love feelings. Recall a real situation in which you were able to comfortably express feelings about your sexual orientation. Where were you? Who were you with? When did this take place?

_____

_____

_____

_____

What was special about this person, time, and/or situation that you think allowed you to feel and believe you were safe?

_____

_____

_____

_____

If, when you think of expressing your same-sex feelings, you can't remember having ever felt safe, what do you think are the obstacles that continue to prevent this?

_____

_____

_____

_____

Looking into your past experiences can give you some ideas about how you can build an internal sense of safety. Remember, you are not a victim, even though you may feel like one at times.

Fear, the Catalyst: Enhancing Your Sense of Safety

Think of fear as your catalyst. If you don't let it inhibit and hurt you, it can give you the push you need to improve yourself and take necessary risks.

Know Your Trigger Fears

If you can identify and challenge your *trigger fears*—the ones that get in the way of feeling safe—you can get on with your life and find out what you're really capable of as a GBQ man. Recognizing your fears isn't always easy, but it can help you understand your feelings and prevent them from interfering with your interpretation of current reality.

Complete the following exercise to help you recognize and challenge your trigger fears:

Examine the following list of characteristics and types of behaviors in other people that may be threatening to you. Check the ones that scare you and make you feel unsafe. Add to the list any behavior or characteristic that causes you to feel threatened or intimidated, to avoid people and situations, or to feel unsafe or scared about your sexual orientation.

_____ Loud talker

_____ Demanding

_____ Angry

_____ Impulsive

_____ Tall or large

_____ Muscular

_____ Men in general

_____ Macho attitudes

_____ "Different" from me

_____ A particular race

_____ People that remind me of _____

_____ _____

_____ _____

_____ _____

_____ _____

Write down how you can deal with the types of people you've checked in the list. Imagine exactly how you can behave—*whenever* they are in your presence or you sense that they will be. (Examples: focus on what I'm there for; leave unobtrusively; remind myself they are not here to hurt me)

_____

_____

_____

_____

Now create another list, this time identifying types of situations (places, environments, etc.) that trigger you to feel threatened. (Examples: unfamiliar places, competitive events, bars)

_____

_____

_____

_____

Write down ways you can deal with the situations you have identified. Try to be specific. (Examples: carry protection; be aware of who is around me) Note that a step-by-step approach to confronting fearful situations is usually helpful.

_____

_____

_____

_____

Stop and check in with yourself. Are your fears warranted in the here and now? Are they relevant and realistic or are they due to specific past encounters that no longer apply? Write out a "reality check" to use as a positive self-talk. (Examples: These are old memories—stay in the present; I'm an adult now and I have choices.)

_____

_____

_____

_____

Now take this exercise one step further and commit to reminding yourself that your fears may be part projection and part reality. One way to tell the difference is to be aware of the masks you put on others and the scenes you create in your head regarding trigger fears. When these masks are in place, when these scenes are playing, you can tell yourself to stop, take a breath, and recognize that you have a choice. You don't have to let these fears control you. You can take an assertive approach instead, by challenging your fears and learning to control them.

Hate Crimes

As I've said before, being a GBQ man is truly an essential part of who you are. Unfortunately, too many GBQ men have been abused in one way or another, and their internal selves are governed by fear; their sense of safety is one big question mark. If you have been traumatized by psychological or physical abuse, you may suffer from an anxiety disorder that prevents you from feeling safe in your world in general—you're always expecting abuse or anticipating situations to be dangerous.

A review of studies related to hate crimes and violence found that 80 percent of gay men and women have been verbally abused, 44 percent have been threatened and 17 percent have been assaulted in some way because of their sexual orientation (Berrill 1992). If you are one of these people, and are experiencing a chronic sense of fear and imminent danger, you will probably benefit from a structured approach to help you conquer your anxiety. Certain cognitive-behavioral forms of psychotherapy and desensitization procedures administered by a trained professional in this area may significantly reduce or eliminate your fear responses caused by traumatic incidents. See the resource section for books and referrals.

Not all people who have been through traumatic experiences develop anxiety disorders. Some GBQ men who have endured brief, mild, or subtle forms of danger may exhibit symptoms including avoidance, fear, nervousness, and low self-esteem. These symptoms may indicate a behavioral or personality-related problem, not an anxiety syndrome.

Finding Internal Support

Support: You may already have it and not know it, or you may know you have it but it's not the kind you want or it's not enough. Or you may know you simply don't have it. Support is a very personal but tangible feeling—you usually know when you feel supported by others and who will be there for you in the best and worst of times. Your task at this point is to look at the kind of support that you need *now*, and what you feel you will need as you work toward opening your identity as a GBQ man.

If you've made it this far (in this book and in life), you are probably aware of which people you have felt safe with and which ones you haven't. You may also have begun to recognize how you can choose to create safety for yourself or continue to live with fear and avoidance, potentially being your own worst enemy.

Are you a "downer" to yourself? Even if you think you're not, imagine what you could do to strengthen your own sense of yourself by becoming your own ally. If you can be your own ally, the support you need can come from within, and you won't need to rely so much on others to provide it for you. Even the most supportive of people will fall short of providing what you need in a relationship if you don't know how to support yourself. Being GBQ *and* self-supporting can be a challenge, but it's a challenge you can face.

Meet Ted, a nice guy of twenty-five who is attractive, funny, and creative. He was struggling to accept his homosexuality and had told only a few people about his feelings. He believed he should not need to reach out to others; to him it was a sign of weakness. Unfortunately, Ted grew up in a family that didn't talk about feelings and that taught him he wasn't supposed to need others. His parents were bright, but critical, and he internalized their criticism, creating self-talk that made it hard to believe he was a generally worthwhile human being. Ted had trouble giving himself credit for his successes and raked himself over the coals when he made mistakes. He continued to deny himself a social life by spending hours on the computer, not introducing himself at functions, avoiding other gay men, clubs, and opportunities for socializing. Ted, needless to say, was not his own ally.

Be Your Own Ally

If you've read this far, you are probably more aware of your internal critic. Like Ted, though, you may need to work more at strengthening your positive self-talk. Regardless of your age or the amount of time you've been out to yourself as a GBQ man, the following exercises can help you identify how to be your own ally. They'll be handy for checking up on yourself and realizing when you're getting in your own way.

Start by identifying the positive and negative poles of your self-talk: supportive and nonsupportive. Think about what you say to yourself about your gay or bisexual feelings, thoughts, or interests. Fill in the table below; it has a couple of examples to get you started.

Negative/Nonsupportive Self-Talk	Positive/Supportive Self-Talk
Being gay is weird.	*My fantasies are exciting.*
I have disappointed my parents.	*I want to be happy as I am.*

Now think of a way you can be more aware of your internal critic and how it impedes your progress as a GBQ man. (Examples: Red-flag my thoughts; The critic keeps me from acting natural.)

_____

_____

_____

Think of a way you can be more aware of your supportive self-talk, and how it helps your progress as a GBQ man. (Examples: Pay attention to when I feel good and notice what I'm thinking, then say it out loud; I'll have more confidence in meeting people I'm really attracted to.)

_____

_____

_____

_____

If nothing else, being honest about being a GBQ man will bring you closer to your true feelings. Use your actions—writing, acknowledging, speaking your truth—to support yourself. Remind yourself that going along with the crowd may be easier, but it doesn't feel as good as doing what is right for you. Give yourself a lot of credit and self-praise for speaking your gay, bisexual, and questioning truths.

Remember Ted? He decided that he would be a lot more relaxed if he were to live his life without having to constantly screen out his same-sex desires. He wanted to start sharing his true feelings when he felt safe enough to do so and letting them go the rest of the time. His motto became "Life is too short to worry about what other people think." His therapist reminded him that most people don't really care about other people's love life, anyway—they're too busy chasing after their own dreams and neuroses! Ted realized nobody but him would get to live his life, and he wanted to live it as a gay man, from then on. To Ted, this new thinking served as a reminder, a relief, and a way to talk back to his internal critic and keep it in check.

If you find yourself being bombarded by critical thoughts or feelings about supporting yourself for being gay or bisexual, try this: Let your mind rest for a moment, and then turn up the volume of those negative voices inside you. Listen, and then list the names of the people to whom these voices seem to belong—a critical parent; an intolerant boss; a priest or pastor from your childhood; a politician.

_____	_____
_____	_____
_____	_____

Imagine putting those critical words and voices into a box and labeled "Trash." Discard the trash, shred it, drop it out of a plane at twenty thousand feet—whatever your heart desires. Don't worry if you think the criticisms have helped you get your work done in the past or improved you somehow, these particular critical voices only masquerade as supporters. They will not help you to be stronger or to challenge yourself constructively.

Now tune into your supportive GBQ voices. They *are* there. These are your allies, your internal support mechanisms. They can be summoned at will. You just have to request their presence. Write down the names of the people to whom these supportive gay and bisexual voices belong. They may be guardian angels or real people in your life; they may have lived in your past but are dead now or may even be figures from history; they may be present in your life right now or somewhere in your hoped-for future.

_____   _____

_____   _____

_____   _____

_____   _____

If it isn't there already, add your own name to the list of allies. If you support yourself in your sexuality or same-sex feelings, then you will lead the way to ongoing support.

What do you want your internal allies to say to you about your sexuality and the different aspects of you as a GBQ man? (Examples: Loving men is following my true heart; Being bisexual is an important part of who I am and how I love; It is my life to live.)

_____

_____

_____

_____

Imagine a verbal skirmish breaking out between your critic and your inner ally. What words would be shouted? How would your ally help you? If you want to take this a step further, write a mental dialogue between your inner ally and your inner critic. Figure out what you will say in support of yourself. For example, Ted wrote this: "Okay, enough of the 'You'll never be a success if you speak your true feelings' bit. My passion for men is okay. I'm not in the dark ages anymore. I want to spend more time with my brother and meet some new friends who will support my career and love interests. And I am a decent-looking guy, too!" Now it's your turn.

_____

_____

_____

_____

Finding Relevant External Support

Who are they and how do you get more of them? I'm not talking about dates. I'm talking about supportive people—other allies to help you through the good times and bad. Just as you looked at your negative critic and positive self-support, explore who your current, real-life negative people are and who your positive allies are (you may already have listed them in the previous exercise). Take a moment to list all the people you feel are "on your side" in life. List others who are not very supportive. For now, let's leave aside the neutral ones.

Positive Allies	Negative People
_____	_____
_____	_____
_____	_____
_____	_____
_____	_____
_____	_____
_____	_____

Create a Community of Your Own

Probably the most common questions I hear from GBQ people are, "How do I meet people in this town?" and "How do I get a date?" But this is not some phenomenon specific to my hometown. It's the same everywhere.

The fact that people's lives are so busy in this technologically driven society has done some damage to the sense of community. People are more mobile and less grounded—geographically and otherwise. They are more fearful of violence and reluctant to rely on others to get things done. They take for granted the necessity of having friends. So let's table the question of how to get a date and focus on how to make friends.

Certainly GBQ men need to have someone to talk to about their same-sex or bisexual feelings as well as their erotic interests. But don't forget common interests like politics, food, movies, music, theater, and all things—superficial and profound—that make life so rich and humorous.

If you don't already have a close friend or two, a neighbor to talk over the fence with, someone to share your cup-a-joe with, it's time to begin building your own support network. I'm not talking about a chat room on the Internet, either, although that may serve some of your need for connections. Most people need at least two good, close friends, as well as a sense of belonging to some kind of community. You may want more than two close friends, for times when everybody seems to be busy, on vacation, or out playing some sport you can't stand.

My closest friends, with whom I can share anything:

_____

_____

_____

_____

The "community" you are connected with may be the universe (a powerful force indeed), West Hollywood, the local gay/bisexual community center, the people in your apartment building, your ethnic group, your choir, or your softball team. Answer the following questions to paint a picture of your community.

Who or what makes up your community at home?

_____

_____

_____

At work/school?

_____

_____

_____

In your family of origin?

_____

_____

_____

From community groups/organizations?

_____

_____

_____

From clubs or teams?

_____

_____

_____

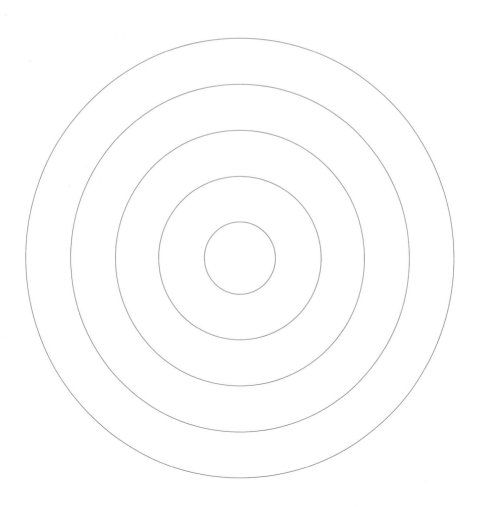

Now take the names or initials of those you've listed above and put them into the preceding diagram of your current social support network. Start with the people closest to you or who know you best, and work from the inner circle to the outer circle, ending with the people who know you least.

Write out who and what you want to be a part of your friendship and community support network. This will be your ideal community.

Imagine how many friends you would like to have and who those friends would be. What kind of support do you want from them? What kind of community do you want to live in? Do you want a racially diverse community? Do you want neighbors to talk to, organizations to be part of? Do you want friends to play ball with or talk with about the latest movie? Would you like to join a support group?

_____

_____

_____

_____

_____

_____

_____

What people can you reach out to who are in your life now? Who do you want to bring into your inner network? Your support community should consist of people who are able to recognize and accept you as a GBQ man. They will be friends you can talk to about the lurid (or not so lurid) details of last night's date who was so full of himself you couldn't get a word in edgewise about your own wonderful self. They will listen to you and tell you when your stories are funny (or boring). They will give you a shoulder to cry on and will just hang out when you want to watch *I Love Lucy* reruns.

_____

_____

_____

_____

_____

_____

If you want, you can go back to the network circle and add in big letters or a different-colored pen the names of people/organizations you want to include in your future. Now take a moment and look back at what you have created. Your next step is to decide how you are going to make this happen. (We'll go to work on that next.) Then make a commitment to work toward it once weekly for the next month.

Strategies for Seeking Support

Here are some common strategies GBQ men have used successfully to build their support network or gain temporary support. Remember, too, that there are plenty of heterosexual people who aren't homophobic and can be an important part of your network. Some of them are probably already in your life. Go ahead and think of some additional ideas that fit for you and your situation and add these to the list.

- Join a support group for gay, bisexual, or questioning men.
- Check out the local gay/lesbian/bisexual community center and see what it has to offer. Volunteer for one of the committees, answer phones, or help with a fund-raiser.
- Volunteer to help at an AIDS support organization.
- Put an ad in the personals of your local free paper to meet GBQ men; list what you want and activities that interest you.
- Join a club or organization that interests you—skiing, biking, hiking, reading, running, country western dancing.
- Take a class—any class.
- Play bingo. (Really!)
- Join a group of GBQ men of your race, religion, or similar ethnic background.
- Join a gay social or political organization.
- Attend a community or Unitarian church that embraces gay members.
- Get on the Internet and access GBQ listings. Look for a chat room for GBQ men.
- _____
- _____
- _____

Obviously, these possibilities for GBQ men will be easier to locate in urban areas or college towns. You may have to search harder if you are not in this type of community. Fortunately, these days you can reach out with a computer and search for what you are looking for. But sometimes the old-fashioned ways are just as beneficial. One way to find support in small towns and rural areas is to find out where the nearest gay bar is. Drop by and snag a few of the free periodicals and event flyers that are usually lying around. Talk to people, including the bartender, to find out what is available for GBQ men in your area.

Distinguishing Needs from Wants

You can't always get what you want, but if you try
sometimes, you just might find, you get what you need.
—The Rolling Stones

It's helpful to differentiate basic needs from wants. Think about what you *need* as being the baseline support system for your safety, psychological survival, and well-being. Consider what you *want* as icing on the cake—a bonus to your basic needs.

The support system you *need* is analogous to food, water, sleep, and exercise. You need them all to keep your body and brain alive and functioning. The support system you *want*, on the other hand, is what you desire to have and strive for beyond your basic survival goals, in the direction of achieving a relationship, close friends, and a community that allows you the freedom to express your GBQ qualities and nature.

Although the distinction between needs and wants may seem somewhat arbitrary, you may find it easier to figure out if you can separate the needs from wants in your self-talk. By identifying your needs and wants, you will also be better able to

- Take responsibility to help yourself when you are struggling with acknowledging your sexuality
- Take care of yourself during tough emotional, financial, career, or social times
- Set goals for yourself
- Deal with self-doubt
- Stand up to prejudice or discrimination
- Clarify your desires for a relationship
- Discuss your feelings with others

As you have learned, safety needs tend to be both physiological and psychological in nature, and support needs can be considered more psychological. This psychological nature of our needs for both safety and support makes the issue somewhat ambiguous and intensely personal. It's something you will have to sort through and clarify for yourself. The following brief exercise may help.

Complete the following sentences, thinking in terms of what you have read in this chapter. Consider what you need or want in relation to your psychological well-being, including comfort, love, security, belonging, okayness, acceptance, and so forth. For example, to feel really safe as a GBQ man you may feel you need to live in a community where there are a lot of other gay or bisexual men around, or where there is little prejudice or religious intolerance of gay/bisexual/racial differences. (Racial prejudice in a community is often accompanied by discrimination against gay and bisexual orientation.) To feel supported, you may need only one good friend and a day-to-day routine that contains occasional supportive events. Or you may be someone who needs to have multiple friends and a strong, active community to rely on.

As a GBQ man, I *need* _____

_____

to feel *safe* in my sexuality and self-expression.

I *want* _____

_____

to feel *safe* in my sexuality and self-expression.

As a GBQ man, I *need* _____

_____

to feel *supported* in my sexuality and self-expression.

I *want* _____

_____

to feel *supported* in my sexuality and self-expression.

When Safety and Support Seem Out of Reach

Though you may find it easy to make a clear choice of a safe, supporting environment, you may not be in a position to make a corresponding move in terms of career or geography. Bear in mind that hard choices must sometimes be made, and you may need to consider such a move if you live or work in a truly oppressive environment. This may mean financial hardships or being away from family or familiar territory—a scary prospect for many.

If your environment is severely oppressive or discriminatory and interferes with your basic sense of survival as a GBQ man, take a moment to imagine what you need for yourself. Try to picture the people around you in your daily life—how they act, what the general environment is like, and what would have to change for you to be comfortable being open as a GBQ man. Write out how this differs from your current living situation. Include what you need to do to institute some or all of the changes necessary to achieve what you envision. If this is not relevant for you, skip this exercise.

_____

_____

_____

_____

_____

_____

If you've completed the preceding exercise and are stuck in a severely oppressive or discriminatory environment, you may have to work at making the changes slowly over several months, or even years. For example, if you are considering a major job or geographic change, it may take a while to find the job or city that meets your requirements. You may need to save some money to move to that gay-positive neighborhood or community you've dreamed of. Be patient—I've seen some persistent men achieve these goals over several years and be glad they stuck it out.

Coming to terms with being gay, bisexual, or questioning means constantly defining and refining your internal and external needs for security and support. I encourage you to continue this process not only as you work through the exercises in this book, but throughout your life.

6

Take Care of Yourself: Spiritual and Emotional Health

We should pray for a sane mind in a sound body.

—Juvenal, *Satires*

In this chapter, you will focus on healing your mind and spirit by looking at some distinct but interconnected parts of your health. You'll explore aspects of your spiritual and emotional well-being that are directly and indirectly influenced by your sexual orientation. In terms of reaching your fullest potential as a healthy, happy GBQ man, you'll need to both focus and integrate your spiritual and emotional energies.

Spiritual Health

In this section, you'll take a look at how your past experiences with religion and spirituality can be exercised or exorcised to build a personal sense of spiritual well-being.

What does spiritual health mean to you?

_____

_____

_____

_____

Religion versus Spirituality

Religion and spirituality are not one and the same. Most people have been raised according to certain religious teachings. For many GBQ men, this *religious* upbringing negatively affected their innate *spirituality*.

The difference between religion and spirituality is often unclear. So let's start by defining them. Though *spiritual* can mean many things, for the purpose of this discussion, we'll concentrate on it as relating to or affecting the spirit. The word *spirit* incorporates meanings ranging from "vital principle" to "soul" to "essence." The word *religious*, on the other hand, usually means faithful devotion to an acknowledged reality or deity, and is associated with words such as "fervent" and "zealous." You can see quite a difference in both sense and tone.

Hawaiian spiritual lore teaches the concept of *mana*, which roughly translates to "spirit energy." It is the power of nature embodied in an object or person. I believe that each man—each GBQ man in this case—must find a way to express his mana. Your way might be through your erotic love, a long-term intimate relationship, a community project, or a political stance for sexual or gender equality. It could also be through the clothes you wear, the words you use, the sports you play, or the way you spend your money. All that you do and say expresses a part of your spirit and connection to the forces of your environment. Whether you choose to express your spiritual beliefs through formal religious prayer or meditation, you can benefit deeply by getting to know and revere your gay spirit, or mana.

Experience suggests that by working to understand and express your own unique thoughts, feelings, and actions as part of your sexual orientation, you'll be better equipped to contribute—by using your mana—to your relationships, your community, and the world at large. No one but you can know what your spiritual energy is. You alone can decide what it will become and what you choose to do with it.

Religious systems that teach you as a child to be ashamed of your natural tendencies for love and physical sensuality can be a source of those bullies and persecutors inside your head. Many GBQ men raised in a religious faith that preaches the "wages of sin" and condemnation of homosexuality have become discouraged, alienated, and shamed by their religion. In fact, a large contingent of GBQ men (and women) consider themselves "recovering Catholics" because they are struggling to overcome the Catholic Church's belief that homosexuality is a sin. The shame and guilt springing from most religious teachings (not only Catholicism) have ravaged the self-esteem and sense of individuality of many a healthy person. And there is no group *more* ravaged than GBQ men attempting to come to terms with their sexuality.

While religions have many beautiful and comforting rituals, in your continuing efforts to honor and respect your sexuality and be true to who you are, I urge you to be willing to recognize the influence that negative religious dogmas have had on you. I encourage you to face and reconcile with your own sense of spirituality. Making peace with your religion and embracing your spirituality are critical steps in escaping the pain of "prejudicial purgatory." Taking these steps will help you quiet, or even end, the battle with your internal homophobe.

Your Religious Upbringing

Ultimately, your spiritual health depends on looking honestly at your past and current experiences with religion and spirituality. By deciding what you consider sacred and by getting to know the aspects of your soul, you give yourself the chance to recapture and embrace an important part of being a GBQ human being. The following series of questions will help you with this examination of your spiritual self:

In general, what was your religious or spiritual upbringing like?

_____

_____

_____

List some teachings and experiences from your religious or spiritual upbringing that you *did* or *do not like*. What do you think their negative effects were? (Examples: The emphasis on guilt and doing bad or sinful things made me fear and be ashamed of my own impulses; Having to dress up, go to the long, boring sermons, and worship in a certain way that did not include me and my individual qualities all kept me from exploring my true spirituality sooner.)

_____

_____

_____

List some teachings and experiences from your religious or spiritual upbringing that you *liked* or *still like*. What do you think their positive effects were? (Examples: The structure gave me a deep sense of being okay and at peace despite the hard times; The holiday celebrations taught me about history.)

_____

_____

_____

Which aspects of your past religion or spirituality do you want to integrate into your current life as a GBQ man? How will you do this? (Examples: I enjoy the sense of community and tradition; I want to continue attending gatherings and benefits to help those in need.)

_____

_____

_____

_____

Which aspects of your past religion or spirituality do you want to eliminate from your current life? (Examples: I don't subscribe to the idea that same gender sex is sinful; I'd like to practice spirituality without having to attend Sunday Services.)

_____

_____

_____

_____

A Healthier Idea of Faith

If you are troubled by your sexuality because of your religious upbringing or simply curious about the prevalent concerns and issues of religion regarding sexual orientation, I encourage you to become better informed. Don't be misled by prejudice. Read, read, read ... and ask questions. If possible, talk with people who have studied religion from different perspectives.

Fortunately, some wise (and nonhomophobic) theologians have thoughtfully examined the scriptures of the Bible and other religious texts and teachings (see the resources section). The more enlightened opinions of these scholars may help you to overcome your internal persecutor. What follows are some useful suggestions from scholarly teachings that will throw a different light on the negative religious teachings you may be struggling to come to terms with.

- *Question the facts.* Examine the bias of judgmental religious teachings past and present. You've most likely heard that the Bible teaches that homosexuality is a sin. The fact is that Jesus mentioned nothing in the New Testament about homosexuality.

- *Consider the source.* Most traditional religious teachings were written by men within a cultural, social context that is now many centuries old. The world was very different then—limited in scope and narrow of view. While writings of long ago contain some good old truths like the Golden Rule, many are ancient and hurtful ideas handed down from generation to generation without consideration for their effects on others.

- *Consider the times.* People of many ages ago were governed by fear and lack of knowledge. They thought the earth was flat and the center of the universe.

- *Be open to different interpretations.* There are many valid interpretations and perspectives of religious writings. For example, a different and more realistic point of view about God's wrath on Sodom and Gomorrah is that it was due to the people's inhospitality and sexual promiscuity in general—not homosexuality.

Here are some other things to consider:

- Gay and bisexual behaviors are found in many aspects of nature, without negative consequences.

- Some faiths have no negative teachings whatsoever about homosexuality. Buddhism, for example, reveres mental and moral self-purification, not a particular sexual orientation.

- Gay and bisexual behaviors have been miscast as a betrayal of procreation and therefore of God, rather than acts of love. They were against the norm, and therefore considered abhorrent because of their unusualness and secrecy. The shame and prejudice grown out of teachings from groups such as Fundamentalist Christians may actually have created and perpetuated a negative set of behaviors by gay and lesbian people. Being forced to hide and lie has further alienated them from society.

- Many traditional religions and societies, including Muslims, Catholics, and Protestants, have discriminated throughout history against women and people of certain races and beliefs—not just against homosexuals and bisexuals.

- Basic tenets of most religions are to treat others with respect, kindness, and caring; and to love and be loved in return. These tenets have nothing whatsoever to do with sexual orientation.

- Being spiritually connected with the forces of a God or other Higher Power has nothing to do with exclusion or discrimination based on sexuality, gender, race, or anything else.

- If AIDS was really "God's punishment" for gay behavior, why are the largest numbers of victims heterosexual, and why are lesbians the lowest risk group?

There are numerous historical examples of gay and lesbian people being honored and incorporated into religious and spiritual life, including the Native American Berdache as medicine man/healer and the marriage ceremonies of same-sex couples in Christianity (Gay Almanac 1996; Boswell

1994). Some current examples of GBQ men taking charge of their spirituality are evident by the thriving numbers of church and other groups that include and are tailor-made for GBQ men and their spiritual needs, such as Roman Catholic Dignity/USA, Evangelicals Concerned, the Unitarian Universalists, and the Radical Faeries, to name a few.

The Rewards of Faith

I have had the good fortune to work with a variety of gay and bisexual people of diverse religious and spiritual beliefs. These lucky ones have found a mature sense of their own personal connection with a religion or spirituality. Whether they believe in Buddhism, Christianity, Judaism, personal spiritualism, or paganism, one thing that resonates in all of these people is a faith, a sense of the interconnectedness among peoples and the Earth. They enjoy a deep trust in themselves and the universe, believing that no matter what happens (rejection from others, prejudice and discrimination, illness, financial hardship, personal and natural disasters), they will be able to transcend the injustice and pain and become stronger from the experience. Also, these faithful folks seem to have developed a gratitude toward life and thankfulness for who and what they have, regardless of the state of their finances, relationships, or health. We're not talking about denial or a Pollyanna approach to living; these people have a deep appreciation for what they have. What do you think about nurturing such an attitude in your life?

How has being a GBQ man helped you to connect more with the spiritual parts of yourself?

_____

_____

_____

Spiritual GBQ men, in particular, may have their spiritual foundations occasionally shaken by external events, but their internal sense of wholeness and health remains intact. In terms of their sexuality, these men have been inoculated against the "dis-ease" of living as a GBQ man in a homophobic world. They have found the individual voice, strength, and sense of well-being that a connection with the spiritual side of life can offer.

Some More Helpful Hints for Gaining Spiritual Well-Being As a GBQ Man

- Many GBQ men are "old souls," with a sense of maturity and uniqueness that's more advanced than other people in their age group. Are you an Old Soul? Do you know one?

- Look for what's sacred in your GBQ love and erotic life.

- You have a special place in this world; tap into your spirit to find it.

- Find spiritual connections. Look for ways to join with individuals, your community, and nature—even if it's only taking a walk in the woods once in a while with a friend.

- Find the miracles in your existence and in the world around you. They're there.

- Sing, dance, create, write, draw, read about spirituality. Use whatever medium you feel comfortable with or interested in, to express experiences that transcend material life.

- Do whatever brings you into the world of spirituality and takes you beyond the humdrum of your daily routine. Put modern society in the closet, for a change.

- Find a place of worship that embraces and accepts GBQ people. (See the resources section in the back of this book.)

There certainly is a lot to explore about yourself and the world when it comes to spirituality. Many GBQ men have learned to view their spiritual health as an essential and ever-developing part of their overall well-being. I encourage you to continue to ponder this idea as you think of your life and coming out as a gay or bisexual man.

Emotional Health

> [A] truly gay-affirmative [Jungian] analyst must be aware of the social and political context in which gay and lesbian patients grew up and now live, for the oppression and intimidation of gay people—which are often the reason they seek help from a therapist—are all too frighteningly, literally real and not just a symbol or fantasy. . . .
>
> —Robert Hopcke, *Same-Sex Love*

As a GBQ man, you face special challenges to your emotional and psychological health. This section focuses on how you can protect and strengthen yourself. You'll also explore the particular contribution your sexual activities make to emotional health.

Developing Resources to Meet the Challenge

As a GBQ man, you may need to regularly provide yourself with some extra psychological fortitude for handling discrimination, prejudice, and resistance to your coming out. This is not to suggest that you walk around watching your back all the time. But it's only realistic to accept that a GBQ man may have to invest more psychological energy than the average heterosexual male to get the support and nurturing he needs. So, it's good medicine to provide yourself with plenty of psychological resources to keep you at your mental and emotional best.

You already have a lot of resources to contribute to your psychological health. Some of them you've learned through your experiences; some you may have learned from friends. You've collected some while working through this book, too, and perhaps from therapy or counseling. All these resources work in unison toward bettering your psychological health.

What have you learned as a GBQ man that makes you emotionally and psychologically healthier? (Examples: I try not to let external acceptance affect my self-esteem as a gay man; Being a GBQ man is one of the qualities that makes me special. And special is good—I am much happier being honest and open about my sexuality.)

_____

_____

_____

_____

Think about the psychological benefits and positive experiences you would have missed out on had you not been GBQ. Write some statements about gratitude and appreciation for your identity, your sexual orientation, and the challenges and passions of being a GBQ man. How can you use this gratitude and appreciation in your daily life to help you through times of negativity and emotional upset?

_____

_____

_____

_____

Psychology of Mind

There are many theories about what contributes to psychological health. A recent form of psychology called *Psychology of Mind (POM)*, or *health realization* (Mills 1995), used as a therapeutic and community approach, has been shown to be particularly useful to maximize mental well-being. Following are some of the health-inducing tenets emphasized by POM. Some cognitive psychotheraputic tenets have been added.

Use Your Innate Mental Health

You possess an innate mental health that can be tapped regardless of circumstances or problems. This innate health will emerge on its own by allowing natural wisdom and intuitive common sense to come to the surface and letting go of judgments that inhibit the natural flow of wisdom. The products of innate mental health include authenticity, inherent creativity, sensitivity to and appreciation of your innermost feelings, and the ability to honor and encourage your uniqueness. The important point here is that little energy is involved in giving the reins to your innate mental health. If you are emotionally wounded, that hurt will heal just as naturally as a flesh wound is healed by your body.

Recognize the Power of Your Thoughts

Your thoughts create your perceptions and reality from moment to moment and are not determined by external factors. If you learn to understand and direct them, you can use your perceptions and thoughts to help you, rather than allowing them to hurt you.

Despite the power of prejudice, discrimination, and stigmatization, as a GBQ man you can focus and realize when you are off track in your thinking. You can notice when you feel bad, sad, guilty, or ashamed, and put yourself on the track of good feelings again, simply by acknowledging that these negative feelings cause you distress. Think about the core beliefs you hold that feed these thoughts and therefore, negative emotional states ("I'm powerless," "People won't love me," "I don't belong"). Think about how you can gently steer your perceptions towards the positive ("I'm being honest with myself and others about my sexual orientation," "I'm getting to know who I am," "I can handle myself").

Stop Stirring the Pot

Negative past experiences do not always have to be "worked through" in order for you to be emotionally and psychologically healthy. Reminding yourself over and over how you have been victimized as a GBQ man, for example, is akin to removing a scab from a wound—it delays the healing process.

Simply noticing the ups and downs of your mood gives you clues as to how your thinking process may have been derailed. Just by observing and acknowledging, "I'm in one of those moods," and not trying to analyze or manipulate the mood, you improve the overall quality of your thinking and experience.

GBQ men are often great analyzers (a survival tactic, no doubt) and feel things very deeply. But try to get out of your own way and just notice what got you off track.

Remember, *your thoughts are just thoughts*, and move on without getting caught up in the drama of your moods. "This too shall pass."

Getting Back on Track

Use the following suggestions, drawn from POM and other positive self-talk strategies to help catch yourself when you're feeling emotionally or psychologically off track. Believe it—you can put yourself back on the healthy track.

- Use your past as a source of new information and added strength— not as a way to criticize yourself and obsess over negative experiences, old resentments, or unresolved worries. Be aware of how core beliefs (called *emotional thoughts*) that were a part of your past memories or experiences affect you. They can have both negative and positive influences on the healthy course of your thinking.

- Life is too short to waste your time worrying. Notice how "worry-time" affects the quality of your thought. Past and future "worry-thoughts" have a way of interfering with the joy of your present time. So, instead of worrying, use your time to solve problems. Experience happiness. Focus on what creates positive feelings. Assert yourself. Be creative and move beyond those old, unproductive fears.

- Recognize that your thoughts create an illusion of reality and affect your behavior. By not reacting to your negative core beliefs as if they were true, you will more effortlessly take responsibility for your behavior.

- Far from soothing the psyche and healing the hurt, poking around and worrying about your past wounds may actually leave you feeling like a victim; and it can prevent emotional wounds from healing.

- Calm your thoughts and emotions by trusting in your innate wisdom. Remain in the here and now, depending on the innate wisdom.

Know that your moods will come and go. This view of healthy thinking is *not* about denying negative feelings or pretending you don't have problems. It's about recognizing that there will be tough times and that you *will* get through them.

Pick a stressful GBQ-related situation (such as fear about coming out to someone or a self-esteem issue related to being GBQ). Over the next week, watch your thoughts and perceptions related to this situation and gently *redirect* them if necessary. Remember to

- Notice your thought process and the power it has to positively or negatively influence your mood

- Discover any core beliefs that interfere with your happiness

- Note how much "worrytime" you spend on past and future issues
- Acknowledge that your thoughts create illusions for you and they have the power to be positive or negative
- Redirect any thoughts that are off track
- Let go of judgments
- Pay attention to the clues your feelings give you about your thinking patterns
- Observe yourself trusting in your own innate health

Write about the results below.

_____

_____

_____

_____

_____

_____

_____

When you put all the suggestions in this chapter together, you'll probably find that you have developed some new and empowering ways to be at your healthy best. Take what you've learned to deepen your overall sense of the positive things in your everyday life.

Stress and Your Overall Health

> *Gay men in general have a greater capacity to cope with stress than heterosexual men, I believe, because throughout their lives they have had to deal with the stress of feeling alienated from mainstream society and have had to find ways to contend with hatred and rejection.*
>
> —Richard Isay, *Becoming Gay*

Research over the past several decades seems to point to a significant relationship between stress (that is, your appraisal of it and how you cope with it) and physical and psychological well-being (Folkman and Lazarus 1984; Goldberger and Breznitz 1993).

Your perception of what is stressful and what is not, is as individual as your fingerprint. Stress as discussed here refers to the *relationship between you and your environment*. You're not simply an object that stands still while the environment and others in it wreak their havoc upon you. Not at all. You're an active participant in the thinking, molding, and interaction of your day-to-day life.

List the events in your current life that you experience as stressful.

_____

_____

_____

_____

Do these stressful events affect your overall sense of mental and emotional well-being? To what extent? What about their influence on your self-esteem as a GBQ man?

_____

_____

_____

_____

How do these stressful events affect your physical health?

_____

_____

_____

_____

How can you reduce the effects of the above stressors? Can you change the way you look at them (this includes accepting them)? Can you change the way you react to them? Can you use some of the health-inducing ideas from POM we discussed in chapter 6?

_____

_____

_____

_____

Changing Your Response to Stress

With the answers to the foregoing questions in mind, look further into the possibility that you can change how you respond to the stressors in your life. The critical piece of the puzzle in this case is *your perception* of the stressful event or relationship. If you perceive the stressor as taxing or exceeding your resources and possibly endangering your well-being, then you will experience psychological stress.

As continually emphasized throughout this book, being GBQ and your response to being GBQ have both direct and indirect influences on your feelings of psychological stress. Your ability to make positive appraisals of your identity, your efforts to cope with shame, guilt, and internalized homophobia, your management of the stresses of coming out, and how you act in a relationship—all of this can reduce or increase your stress.

For example, if you cope with your bisexual identity by feeling ashamed, keeping your sexual identity and interests hidden, and avoiding meeting peers and potential partners, you may be creating stress for yourself. The stress may manifest itself as uncomfortable feelings and behaviors; reinforced, and even increased, guilt and shame; anxiety about being "found out"; and isolation from supportive people in your life. In contrast—and as supported by many of the individual examples in this book—a healthy, open, and self-esteem-enhancing approach to your sexual orientation is the way to go. Being honest and authentic generally reduces psychological stress and helps you feel good about you and your life as a GBQ man.

Answer the following questions to zero in on the stress in your life.

In your current life, what events, actions, or relationships that are directly related to being a GBQ man cause stress? What would you change? (Example: My relationship with my boyfriend is sometimes tense because of how uncomfortable he is with being open about his sexual orientation. Change? Discuss with him how I feel about this and what I want to change. That way we can work together to improve his comfort level with being out and clarify when each of us may not want to be out.)

_____

_____

_____

_____

What type of behavior do you engage in that adds to the stress of being GBQ? What would you change? (Example: I try to act 'straight' and fit in. Change? Be me, dress like me, and care more about being true to me.)

_____

_____

_____

_____

What thoughts do you have that add stress to being a GBQ man? What would you change? (Example: I think others are watching and judging me negatively because of my sexual orientation. Change? Notice my paranoid thinking, realize I'm off the healthy thought track, and realize it's how *I* feel about *myself* that's important.)

_____

_____

_____

_____

How do your emotions as a GBQ man create stress and what would you change? (Example: I have anxiety and fear of others finding out that I'm gay. I worry about how they will react. Change? Learn some in-the-moment stress reduction techniques like deep breathing. Keep a journal to clarify my feelings and notice how my thoughts affect my emotions.)

_____

_____

_____

_____

Remember to HALT

Whether you're single or not, the demands of today's high-tech, high-energy pursuit of the good life create a tendency for people to try to be it all. Members of Alcoholics Anonymous and other twelve-step programs have a helpful saying: "Don't let yourself get too Hungry, Angry, Lonely, or Tired." They remember it with the buzzword *HALT*. It's a good reminder about the importance of taking care of yourself every day, not just in times of stress. Make sure your basic human needs for nourishment—both physical and mental—are met most of the time. These things seem very simple, but people tend to forget them, no matter now bright, sophisticated, and successful they are. Getting enough sleep, exercising, following a healthy diet, and pursuing a reasonable dose of companionship from other people really do help you to deal with the stress of life as a GBQ man.

7

Questioning Questions
and Finding Answers

*Eventually I not only came to terms with being a gay man,
but I came to recognize that I loved being one, and want to
be no other. That's been, and continues to be, a miraculously
wonderful coming of age.*

—Larry Kramer, writer and activist

In this chapter, you will explore the questions and doubts you may still
have about being a GBQ man. In the process, you will look at your own
beliefs about nature versus nurture, coming out, and homophobia.

Being Consciously
Out to Yourself

It is hard sometimes in today's society to be unique, but by acknowledging to yourself who you are as a GBQ man, and by learning to accept
your real self, you can inoculate against whatever discrimination and
prejudice is keeping your real self in the closet. When you are comfortable
and accepting of your sexual orientation, you will be out to yourself.
Then coming out to others will be easier and more natural; it will become
a comfortable way of sharing who you are. Use this as your mantra:
"From the inside out."

Cal thought that all he had to do to feel good about himself was come out as a bisexual man to his friends. If they accepted him, he thought, he would be more comfortable with his bisexuality. Cal discovered, however, that he hadn't really acknowledged some of his own internal doubts about whether it was okay to be bisexual and that he must first accept himself before he went looking for outside approval.

Question Your Questions

Does the nature-versus-nurture question haunt you? Do you ask yourself, "Where did my sexual orientation come from?" If so, your worries are almost certainly keeping you from being comfortable with and accepting of your sexual orientation and interests. You're going to have to be patient with yourself and prepared to do a lot of hard work toward changing.

Age-old, obsessive, stress-inducing, answerless questions like "Why am I gay?" or "What caused me to be bisexual?" are sure to damage your self-esteem and lead you on an endless chase. These types of questions can loop you silly. They contribute to feelings of hopelessness and make you feel victimized, keeping you from taking responsibility for your life and moving forward on a goal-directed, positive path. Nevertheless, it may help to take just a moment and answer—truthfully—the following questions. It may help you to know what keeps you stuck.

If I knew for sure that I am gay/bisexual because of biological, psychological, or environmental factors, would I change my sexual orientation? How?

_____

_____

_____

_____

Why does it matter to me where my sexuality came from? Will having an answer make me feel more validated or secure about who I am?

_____

_____

_____

_____

Is my concern about the source of my sexuality due to something I feel ashamed of or guilty about?

_____

_____

Would it make a difference if it were completely okay with society or my culture to be gay or bisexual?

Are the concerns identified here influencing you to continue questioning your orientation? In what ways?

What can you do about the negative influences and judgments that you have internalized or that still are active in your life?

Handling Your Questions
Is Biology Responsible?

Homosexuals do not make a voluntary or intellectual decision to be erotically attracted toward, and to fall in love with, someone of the same sex. The propensity to do so is something that reveals itself, in much the same way as a dream reveals itself.

—J. Money, *Gay, Straight, and In-Between*

Research has shown that, when comparing identical versus fraternal twins, male and female bisexuality and homosexuality are "moderately inheritable" (Bailey 1995). For example, Pillard and Weinrich (1986) found that 52 percent of identical twins, where at least one twin is gay or bisexual, were both gay or bisexual. The moderate level of genetic correlation suggests that environmental factors must also be involved. As yet, however, no single or group of biological or socioenvironmental factors have been identified as determining whether someone will be gay, bisexual, or heterosexual. (For a good review of these issues see: Bohan 1996.)

Large population studies have not yet been done on gays and lesbians. In any case, such studies may not ever pin down the exact nature of sexual orientation—not in our lifetime, anyway. Studies have examined genetics, brain structure (such as the size of the hypothalamus), and endocrinology as possible deciding factors in sexual orientation. But most of this work has been methodologically insufficient (due to small or biased population samples) to either support or deny the biological theories. Some people see these studies as potential sources of evidence in "the case for" bi- or homosexuality being something you do not have a choice about. Others see such evidence as akin to a wave of discrimination, supporting the perception of bi- and homosexuality as a defect.

Ask yourself this: Does it matter to me whether being bi and gay is biological (genetic, in utero, etc.) or not? Why does it matter to me?

_____

_____

_____

_____

If biology versus choice is an issue for you, you might want to look further into why. Think about this some more and write about it in your journal. You just might uncover some core beliefs that have created certain insecurities or doubts you have about your sexual orientation. Your need to know whether being gay or bisexual is biology or not might stem from your own uncertainty. Ultimately, the biology-versus-choice debates seem to be an attempt to justify something that really needs no justification. But let's examine the issue a bit further to help you with any nagging doubts you may have about environmental influences on your sexual orientation.

Is My Upbringing Responsible?

Have you ever wondered if environmental factors have caused you to be gay or bisexual? Questions like this often hover in the back of many GBQ men's minds. And unless they get answered in one form or another, the questions will stay there, continuing to create self-doubt and self-hatred. These unanswered questions can foster the fear of being exposed and a nagging sense that it is somehow wrong to be gay or bisexual.

Many of my GBQ clients, when pressed to talk about some of their own self-doubts, reveal that they have considered that their sexuality may be the result of something that happened while they were kids. If this is not the case for you, congratulations. Nevertheless, I still encourage you to work through the following questions to see if there is any inkling of self-doubt.

What did you learn about men, women, life, and sex that you think may have contributed to your being gay?

_____

_____

_____

_____

Do you think your parents contributed in some way to your sexual orientation or feelings? If so, how?

_____

_____

_____

_____

Do you feel a specific incident in your childhood influenced your sexual orientation? If so, what was the incident and how has it influenced you?

_____

_____

_____

_____

What other environmental factors do you suspect may have contributed to your being gay or bisexual?

_____

_____

_____

_____

Now look at your answers to these questions. Is what you've written about unique to you, or is this true of other GBQ men you know? Do you know heterosexual people with some of the same environmental influences?

_____

_____

Think about rephrasing the foregoing questions so they might be asked of a heterosexual person. Do they seem ludicrous when directed toward a straight person? If they do, it won't be difficult for you to accept that your culture and society have taught you that heterosexuality is okay, while homosexuality is considered abnormal. Heterosexuality, then, is automatically considered good, right, moral, natural, and so on. Because of this, many gay and bisexual people in Western cultures are often quick to condemn themselves.

I have asked many a GBQ client, "If it's true that your father (or mother) was absent, domineering, ineffectual, unaffectionate, or harsh, so were many other parents of heterosexual people in our society. Why did *they* turn out to be heterosexual and not homosexual?" Or I may ask of a GBQ man who has been sexually molested, "If you were molested by a man, why didn't that make you want women more?" Or, "If you were molested by a woman, why didn't that sexualize you to be interested in women?" Molestation does not determine sexual orientation, and neither does a parent's treatment.

Am I Defective?

Let's move now to thoughts you may have had that your gay or bisexual orientation somehow means you're psychologically disturbed or defective. Going all the way back to the famous Evelyn Hooker study (1956), in which she studied gay men and compared the results of their psychological tests to those of heterosexual men, finding no difference between the two groups, other studies have failed to find differences between the psychological health of gay and heterosexual men. If you are concerned about poor mental or emotional health simply because you are gay, bisexual, or questioning, ask yourself the following questions:

What in my experience has led me to believe that being gay or bisexual means I'm sick?

Why am I being negative and judgmental in these ways about being GBQ?

_____

_____

Have I bought into harmful stereotypes about gay and bisexual people? In what way?

_____

_____

_____

_____

Despite common assumptions to the contrary, the percentage of gay and bisexual men who are disturbed or dysfunctional is not any larger than the percentage of heterosexual men who are disturbed or dysfunctional. Am I hanging out with or being exposed to only a certain segment of the gay and bisexual population, leading to disproportionate negative judgments?

_____

How can I be more accepting of my sexuality, regardless of its source?

_____

_____

_____

_____

Homophobia and You

Homophobia is one of those words that's been overused and perhaps even trivialized. Homophobics include the teenager next door who spray-paints "FAG" on your fence and the Bible-toting televangelist who preaches that being gay is a sin. Homophobia is implicit in the "Don't ask, don't tell" policy of the U.S. military.

Fear of same is a literal translation of homophobia. The dictionary defines it as an "unreasoning fear of or antipathy towards homosexuals and homosexuality." What does homophobia mean to you?

Start by writing your general definition of homophobia.

_____

_____

Homophobia includes prejudice of any kind based on sexual orientation. Obvious examples include hate crimes, such as gay bashing; threats and name calling; rejection from military service; and denial of the viability of gay or bisexual relationships. Less easily proven but just as unjust is discrimination in hiring, firing, and promotion decisions in the workplace, and in real estate transactions and housing rentals. Other examples are general stereotyping and omitting gay partners from family affairs.

Describe an example of homophobia in your life.

_____

_____

_____

_____

There is little doubt that you live in a heterosexual-dominant society, and it remains to be seen how much your culture will be able to wise up and grow up. You may have noticed how much more common it is these days to see GBQ people on television and in movies, to read about gay/bi issues in the print media, to access gay and bisexual issues in cyberspace. This relatively newfound "external acceptance" won't always offer you internal comfort and acceptance, however—although it sure does help ease the pain of not belonging. Society in general is still a long walk from accepting gay and bisexual people as equal, moral, and respectable citizens, and you may be perpetuating such beliefs in yourself.

Internalized homophobia is that personal fear, shame, and guilt you may have about being gay or bisexual. Internalized homophobia is characterized by

- Negative self-statements
- Avoidant behaviors
- Denial that you're GBQ
- Self-hatred
- Disgust over your sexuality or interests
- Irritation or defensiveness about gay or bisexual leanings

You may never speak of it. You may never even think of it. You may not even realize it is in your life. Most GBQ men experience internalized homophobia to one degree or another, especially in the early phases of coming out. It can happen to you, no matter what your developmental level, and you need to be ready to cope with it.

Coming face-to-face with internalized homophobia may occur as you encounter various developmental and life challenges and the stresses that accompany them, such as getting older, committing to a life partner, changing jobs, losing a loved one, moving to a new city, buying a house, or having a physical illness. Some of these issues may threaten your self-esteem and ruffle the feathers of your identity. Homophobia is a fear, and the degree to which it shakes you will depend on how secure or insecure you are. It will be influenced, as well, by the opinions of your family of origin, unavoidable negative messages from society, and a self-identity that is not yet solidified.

Even men who are supposedly "comfortable and out" may exhibit internalized homophobia in the way they treat themselves. The hallmarks are self-destructive sexual behavior, substance abuse, sarcasm, anger, and shame—a lot of what we have already explored in this book. Internalized homophobia can affect your friendships, love relationships, sexual relations, family bonds—in general, everything in your life that is touched by your identity and self-esteem.

Am I Homophobic?

Peter had been out as a gay man since age eighteen, when he left home after graduating from high school. Now, fifteen years later, after his lover ended their long-term relationship, he was in a slump of self-doubt about his sexuality. He avoided his gay friends. He began to think there was something wrong with being a gay man; he focused on his Catholic upbringing and how his parents had shamed him. He became more and more irritable and unwilling to date new people.

What are the signs of your internalized homophobia? Look for feelings of shame, fear, avoidance, irritation, and anger.

_____

_____

_____

_____

Peter had started to pull away from old friends and judge their actions harshly. He had isolated himself at work more, disclosing less about his life. He judged himself and his actions harshly, and had lost his previous joy in his erotic attraction to men.

How does your internalized homophobia affect your relationships? Work? Sex life? Spiritual life? Acceptance of your ethnic heritage? Self-esteem?

_____

_____

_____

_____

For each of the areas you've just identified, think about what you'd like to change. Peter, for instance, wanted to be close with his gay friends again. He needed to regain his positive approach at work and to have a few friends there in whom he could confide. He also wanted to enjoy dating and sex again.

In terms of internalized homophobia, what would you like to change

In your relationships?

_____

_____

_____

At work?

_____

_____

_____

In your sex life?

_____

_____

_____

About your self-esteem?

_____

_____

_____

In your spiritual life?

_____

_____

_____

About your acceptance of your ethnic heritage?

_____

_____

_____

Go through the following list of possible ways to eliminate your internalized homophobia and loosen the blocks to your self-acceptance as a GBQ man.

- Change my church or denomination
- Change the way I view or practice my spirituality
- Stand up and speak out against negative judgments
- Develop positive self-talk to challenge myself and create new messages about my sexuality
- Reconnect with my gay and bisexual friends
- Read about the biology of sexual attraction and orientation
- Read more about gays and bisexuals in history and in the world today
- Talk to people who are supportive and affirming of gays and bisexuals
- Get to know other GBQ men of my race, ethnicity, or culture
- Get to know and develop closer relationships with more gay and bisexual people
- Find gay and bisexual people to have as positive role models
- Keep a journal of my feelings and doubts
- Develop methods and rituals of affirming myself as a GBQ man
- Participate in GBQ community events
- Begin therapy or join a GBQ-positive support group
- _____
- _____
- _____

Now, write down at least one other way that you can eliminate your internalized homophobia or improve your positive sense of being GBQ. Peter, for instance, wanted to feel better about himself as a gay man, but was confused. He decided to read some gay-positive books and to journal his feelings, which helped him face some of his self-doubts. He reconnected with some gay friends and slowly began to date again.

What changes will you make?

_____

_____

_____

_____

_____

_____

_____

Clinical experience and research show that the ability to accept one-self (regardless of society's prejudices) overwhelmingly contributes to positive adjustment in life and society. This is essentially what we all must do, regardless of our sexual orientation, to feel confident and united in the various aspects of ourselves. As GBQ men especially, we must be willing to constantly come out to ourselves, face ourselves, show up for ourselves. When we can stand up and be present in the moment, accepting who were are now and as we change and evolve, we foster an ongoing positive development of ourselves and our GBQ identity.

8

To Come Out or
Not to Come Out

I knew I would gradually have to come out regardless of the consequences. Those consequences have at times been quite heavy, but nothing has been as important as the freedom being out has given me.

—Richard Isay, *Gay Souls*

The self-examination you've done in this book so far will serve you well in this chapter, in which you'll add yet another layer to your under-standing of yourself so that you can make the decision to come out. This chapter also offers guidelines and tools for understanding your own ex-pectations and motivations to come out to others. Whether you have yet to come out to anyone or are thinking of coming out to someone new in your life, this chapter will help you.

Coming Out:
A Personal Matter

Decisions about coming out are ultimately decisions only you can make for yourself. Before you go any further, review the basic ideas about what it means to come out (Hunter 1996):

Coming out as a GBQ man means

- Recognizing and acknowledging yourself as gay, bisexual, or questioning

- Learning information about the gay or bisexual community

- Disclosing your sexual orientation to others, including family, friends, peers, and colleagues

- Becoming more comfortable with and accepting your sexual orientation

Keep in mind that coming out is both an internal and an external process. Coming out is more than just telling others about your sexual orientation; it's knowing and feeling the truth *and* it's saying it out loud. Because of the work you've done in this book so far, you're well on your way to fortifying your identity as a GBQ man. Now it's time to make a decision about who else needs to know.

If you continue to be unsure about your sexual orientation, that's okay, don't despair. You may still be in the "questioning" part of the GBQ definition, and it may take some more time to clarify your true feelings and needs. Keep in mind if you are still questioning that clarification will come as a result of overcoming your fear of being judged by others, your shame and guilt about being "different," and any internalized homophobia you may be dealing with. And don't forget the importance of talking with safe, supportive friends or consulting an informed, gay-positive therapist. Getting help and support will save you a lot of grief and confusion about your same-sex or bisexual feelings and thoughts. Coming out and being out have stages and phases just like any other part of life. You will have to figure out for yourself where you are in these coming-out stages and where the stages fit into your individual development.

As you work through this chapter, remember that

- Being *internally* comfortable with your orientation will help you be more at ease sharing your sexual orientation with others. You'll be stronger in the face of whatever negative reactions you encounter as a result of coming out.

- Coming out to others will reinforce your pride as a gay or bisexual man. You'll be able to express the *external* aspects of your sexuality and participate in the gay and bisexual community.

- Coming out to others will help you identify the supportive people in your life—those who truly accept and care about you.

How Your HIV Status Affects Your Coming Out

If you are HIV-positive, it may be even harder to come out about your sexuality. You may feel as though you are faced with outing yourself twice. It helps to remember that you only have to come out to the people you are ready to tell. You don't have to tell everyone everything; you don't even have to tell *anyone* everything. It's up to you to selectively share your status, depending on how close you are or want to be with the individual.

Your HIV-positive status forces you to cope with complex feelings and intense emotions, such as grief and fear. These emotions, and the issue of your mortality, will be part of your coming-out process. As a man living with HIV, you may also need more or different kinds of support in the coming-out process; if you haven't joined one already, you may want to find an HIV support group.

The discussions and exercises in this chapter, for the most part, are applicable whether you are gay, bisexual, or questioning, regardless of your HIV status.

Some Coming-Out Stories

After his first year in college, Alan decided to visit his sister across the country and he wanted to bring along his new partner. Alan and his sister had never talked about his being gay, yet they've been close since they were kids. When he called her to tell her he wanted to visit, he said, "It's important you know I have a boyfriend now." He sensed that she was somewhat uncomfortable, but she was open to talking about it. To give her time and space to assimilate her feelings, Alan and his lover decided to visit as planned, but to stay in a hotel near his sister's house.

> Note that the word *questioning* as we've used in GBQ eventually won't apply as you come out as gay or bisexual.

Joe is twenty-four and lives in New York City. When he found out he was HIV-positive, he decided to come out to his parents. He wanted to tell them he was bisexual first and wait to talk to them about his HIV status. He mulled over how and when to tell them, but knew it was important for him to do it. He finally wrote them a letter. They called right after reading it and were, to his amazement, very supportive. He had expected them to be judgmental as they were strict Catholics. He had decided to tell his sister first about his HIV status and get her advice about when to tell their parents about his health.

Kevin, a fifty-six-year-old Methodist minister from the Southwest, wanted to come out to his colleagues. He considered the risks versus the rewards of coming out and had decided it was important for him to do it at that time in his life. He wrote out each of his colleague's names and, next to their names, why he cares enough about each of them to tell the truth. He decided to share his writings and talk with them about it at an upcoming retreat.

Mark is a thirty-five-year-old, bright, career-minded corporate manager. He wanted to be able to bring his partner of five years to work-related social functions and to be more comfortable at work when talking about his private life. He was tired of hiding. On a professional level, he wanted his company to implement domestic partner benefits. After looking at the company's policy on discrimination (there was a sexual orientation discrimination clause), he started telling close colleagues. He brought a picture of his partner to put on his desk and truthfully answered questions about the photograph from interested co-workers. He decided to bring up the issue of domestic partner benefits at the next department meeting.

Don had mixed feelings about his high-school years. He had been close to his friends on the soccer team and fondly remembered a few girls he had dated. He also feared and hated certain guys who pushed their physical strength and heterosexual prowess around. While attending his twentieth high-school reunion, Don decided to write about his male partner and out himself as gay in the "What I'm doing now" section of the reunion book. He proudly brought his partner to the formal dinner and ceremonies, and they danced all night long.

These are some bold coming-out stories about men with a lot of courage. They represent possibilities and offer hope. The consequences of these events were not always positive and the situations required thoughtful handling. With the help of this book, you will create your own stories about when and how to come out, keeping in mind your goals, motives, and decisions about whether you can live with the potential ramifications of being genuinely out in each situation along your road of life.

Revisiting What Coming Out Means to You

Look back at your response in chapter 1 to the question, "What does the coming-out process mean to you?" and answer the following questions:

How has your understanding or experience of the coming-out process changed?

_____

_____

_____

_____

What revelations have you had that you would pass on to other GBQ men who started where you did in the process?

_____

_____

_____

What have you learned so far that you can use to support your unique and changing needs?

_____

_____

_____

_____

Expectations and Motivations

An important part of examining what coming out means to you is to think about your expectations of what will happen, and your purpose or motives for coming out.

Whether you're coming out for the first time or you're simply coming out to someone new, what do you expect will happen? How do you think your life will change (in general and in terms of specific people or circumstances)?

_____

_____

_____

_____

_____

Have your expectations and motivations changed since you began reading this book? How?

_____

_____

_____

Your expectations will not always match what really happens, especially when it comes to other people's reactions. But the value you place on coming out and the benefits you expect to reap are vital to the process. That is, if you're clear about your reasons or motivations for coming out and you commit to being authentic with yourself and others, you will come closer to living up to your expectations.

Frank, for example, came from a background of abuse in both his family and peer environments. As an adult, he made a conscious choice to break out of his "victim" cycle. He created a supportive environment for himself, full of friends and allies. He made a conscious commitment to value being authentic, including being open about his sexuality. As a result, he developed a set of expectations and lifetime goals that included friendships, lovers, and acquaintances who would treat him with respect and value him for all of his different qualities. Frank therefore overcame his internal "script" of expectations that dictated he would always be a victim. He now expected motivated to be authentic and made sure he created friendships with people who appreciated him and treated him well.

Be Realistic

When you defined your expectations in the previous section, did you write down all positives or all negatives? If you did either, you may be setting yourself up for a fall or sabotaging your coming-out process. Be aware of your expectation pattern and be willing to balance it out. Anticipating all negative responses may be the result of a negative mind-set ("Bad things always happen to me"); poor self-esteem ("I don't deserve for people to accept me"); significant negative past experiences ("People abused me as a child"); or fear ("I'm afraid being out as a GBQ man will cause people to reject me"). While it's realistic to expect some negative responses, look at all the possibilities of your coming out. If you wrote only negatives, go back and try to add an expectation of something positive that can happen if you come out. Clinical experience and research have revealed that, generally speaking, if you have a can-do attitude and expect positive results, the actual outcome will be more positive.

Why Tell?

Exploring some of your motivations for telling others will help you better clarify your specific reasons for coming out to some people. Not that you *have to* come up with reasons for disclosing anything about yourself. This is simply another way for you to think through your coming out. See if any of the following motivations for coming out to people in your life apply to you (Cain 1991). Jot down names or situations after the ones that sound familiar:

- Therapeutic disclosure (to enhance self-esteem and seek support to deal with stigma)

- Relationship-building disclosure (to improve closeness with others)

- Problem-solving disclosure (to resolve situational problems created by secrecy about being GBQ)

- Preventative disclosure (to prevent potential problems from emerging)

- Spontaneous disclosure (unplanned revelations in response to feelings of comfort or safety or opportune moments with others)

- Political disclosure (to make GBQ issues more visible, change attitudes, provide models, or offer support to the community)

You may want to use these categories as guideposts to your decision-making process in coming out. Remember though, you needn't always have a reason for being open and authentic.

Identifying Your Specific Expectations

Hank, a forty-three-year-old corporate businessman, had never come out to his family. He'd once been married to a woman for a year, but had always known deep inside that he was gay. He'd been involved with three men in his life, including one whom he loved deeply and lived with for two years. Hank was quite scared to tell his large Catholic family about his sexual orientation. He was sure he would be disowned and ridiculed by his family members, though he hoped the one exception would be his "liberal-minded" sister. Hank decided to tell only the family members he wanted to tell. He started by telling a trusted cousin, but word leaked out and soon everyone in the family knew Hank was gay.

Hank learned about the law of averages from his experience: One-third of his family thought it was no big deal; one-third was incredibly supportive and caring; and one-third was either undecided or very uncomfortable with the fact that he was gay. To Hank's surprise, his "liberal-minded" sister was included in the uncomfortable group. However, contrary to his expectations, no one in his family disowned him or hated him.

Hank's story is not uncommon. I'm sure that you also have expectations about the results of coming out to your loved ones. You may expect, as many people often do in anxious situations, that the worst will happen. Or you may not want to feel the disappointment if things don't go well, so you expect things to be difficult instead of getting your hopes up. Then again, you may be one of the eternal optimists who take it for granted that everything will work out fine. Your general anticipatory style will color your coming-out process. The best thing to do is to use a reality-based coping strategy: just accept what happens as being beyond your control; know you have to do what you have to do regardless of others' opinions.

Pick a specific person to whom you would like to come out and answer the following questions. You'll identify how you feel right now about coming out to this person and what you expect will happen as a result.

When you think about coming out to _____ , how do you feel *right now*? Circle the ones that apply and add whatever other feelings you have.

Afraid	Relieved	_____
Pleased	Curious	_____
Confused	Excited	_____
Embarrassed	Nervous	_____

When you think about coming out to _____ , what do you *expect* will happen?

I'll feel relieved.

He or she will tell me some inner secrets, too.

He or she will reject my sexuality but will still like me.

I won't have to pretend anymore when I'm around him or her.

I'll feel more comfortable speaking freely about myself and my life.

I don't know.

I'll become closer to him or her.

He or she will judge me.

He or she will accept me unconditionally.

I'll just feel more comfortable in general.

I'll be able to let him or her know more about me.

_____

_____

_____

Now stop and examine your expectations. What, if anything, did or can you learn about yourself from them?

_____

_____

_____

First and foremost, recognize that these expectations are *your perceptions*; they can create or influence your reality (see chapter 6). That is to say, if you're expecting someone will accept you as a GBQ man, you may act in some ways that encourages (through your eye contact, confidence, tone of voice, or body language) the person to listen and accept who you are more easily. Achieving a match between what you expect and the actual results depends on how you present yourself and your ideas, how realistic your expectations are in general, and how open-minded others are (such as a sibling who says, "You can never bring your kind into my house").

Remember that the results you expect may or may not happen; the outcome is not completely in your control, because you simply can't control other people's reactions.

A Few Pointers about Your Expectations and Motives

Now examine your motives; you can learn from them, too. Who or what is going to benefit from your coming out? If you are coming out primarily as a way to help or improve yourself, and secondly to benefit a relationship, you will have an easier time of it. This is because you are doing it for *you*, rather than depending on others for approval. Don't get me wrong—wanting to share your sexuality and improve intimacy between you and other people in your life is a valuable goal. But coming out is an act of love for *you* over and above all others.

If you expect others will want to get to know you now that you have come out or they will want to be closer because of your honesty, then go for it—slowly. Coming out to friends, family, and peers may actually knock down some barriers to intimacy and bring you closer. You will have achieved what you expected and hoped for. On the other hand, coming out sometimes results in shock or surprise. Some people may suddenly feel they don't know you anymore. As a result, they may distance themselves from you rather than moving closer to you (at least, initially). Your friends, family, or work colleagues may have negative feelings about bi- or homosexuality (or any kind of sexuality!) that you or even they were not aware of. If this is the case, remember that you are still the same person you were before you told them (maybe a little braver). Their judgments about these matters have nothing to do with your value as a person.

When coming out to yourself and others, you may feel a sense of being more connected, more spiritual, and more loving, and naturally you'll want to share this exuberance with others. However, sometimes you may feel coming out is a bit of a burden. Sharing intimate feelings that are not "culturally sanctioned" can be hard work. Nevertheless, negative and positive feelings won't always mesh with how others think or feel. It may take a while for their sense of who you are to settle in. While it can be exhilarating to share your own excitement about your inner passions and newfound self, don't expect others to always share your feelings. I urge you to find people who will indeed share your excitement, but understand that some of your friends, peers, and family will take a while to accept your sexual orientation. At worst, you will have to let some of the people in your life go, despite your closeness in the past.

Creating a Response Style for Yourself

Fill in the following sentences using your own words. For ideas, go back and look at what you wrote in the exercise about defining your expectations. If you get stuck, pick a behavior that applies to you from the list on the following page.

My usual way of reacting to emotionally charged situations is

_____

_____

_____

I think I will react to coming out by

_____

_____

_____

Instead, when I come out to _____ (or in general), I want to

_____

_____

_____

Response Behaviors

- Run like hell in the opposite direction

- Withdraw; become more quiet

- Face it head on and do what I have to do

- Look at my options and then respond

- Not be ruffled by others opinions of me

- React from my gut; no holds barred

- Share whatever comes to my mind

- Talk about my feelings and decide what I want

- Practice what I want and then act

With the preceding facts about yourself in mind, you can begin to develop a different approach to emotionally charged situations like coming out. Specifically, you must learn to *respond* instead of *react*. What's the difference? A little thoughtfulness. *Reactions* are physiological, instinctive behaviors; *responses* are similar to reactions, but you add the step of thinking about your feelings, the other person, or the situation. Did you discover in the exercises that you are the type of person who acts on your gut feelings? If so, I encourage you to respond instead— to be thoughtful about your behavior. In terms of coming out that means thinking ahead about the who, what, and when.

This does not mean you should analyze every detail about what you will do. And don't waste time and energy predicting other people's reactions. Remember Hank—he thought his "liberal" sister would be accepting of his sexual orientation; yet she ended up being one of the most uncomfortable. Sometimes people expect certain reactions from others despite the fact that this is beyond their control. But you *can* expect yourself to come out in the way you want to, regardless of how others react.

As you move through your coming-out process, continue to remind yourself of these things:

- You are not alone.

- Telling your truth is the right thing to do.

- Responding instead of reacting increases your ability to understand and get what you want.

- Predicting how others will react may sometimes be a good survival strategy, but it is often inaccurate; it can create unnecessary fear and get in the way of accomplishing your goals.

- Don't take it personally if someone reacts negatively to your sexual orientation. Remember, it's says more about them than you.

Better Safe Than Sorry

If you suspect violence could be a reaction to your coming out to a particular person, you'll need to realistically assess that situation. Or if you think there is a good chance that you will jeopardize basic survival needs, such as your job or your home, you would probably be better off not coming out. Sometimes there is value in the motto "Better safe than sorry."

People with a history of violent or abusive behavior or with strong judgments about sexual orientation may not be the best people for you to come out to. For example, a financially dependent teenager living in a right-wing, Fundamentalist household may want to think twice about coming out to his parents, and so might the employee whose boss discriminates against a certain race or gender (bigotry is bigotry). For these people, there may be much to lose, including their housing, physical well-being, or basic financial security.

More often than not, though, anxiety can make a mountain out of a molehill. My experience has been that people are often more accepting than we assume. Of course, this depends on who it is you want to tell, where you live, the prevailing cultural climate, and how the other person feels about homosexuality. Again, only *you* can really know what is relatively safe. Just remember that coming out is not without its risks, no matter how much you think about it or try to plan for it.

Who? What? When?

Coming out is a process, an everyday process at that. If you're newly discovering your sexual orientation, you may be feeling that you're making these coming-out decisions at every turn. Even if you've been out for a while, you still may be faced with these decisions and you still need to work on preparing yourself.

First, let's find out what you already know. If one of the following questions doesn't apply to you, skip it and move on to the next one. Your answers will help you analyze what coming-out experience you already have available.

When did you first realize you might be GBQ? How old were you?

How long have you been out to yourself? That is, how long have you acknowledged you are GBQ?

How old were you when you first told someone you were GBQ?

To whom did you first come out? _____

_____

What made you decide to come out to that person? _____

_____

What helped you to come out to that person? _____

_____

If you answered any of the preceding questions, then you already have some experience you can draw from, even if you feel you didn't handle the situation well at the time.

Whom Do You Want to Tell?

In my clinical practice, I've found that many GBQ men feel empowered by making well-thought-out decisions about the people to whom they want to come out. Such careful consideration will allow you to

- Respond instead of react
- Honor your commitment to being real, passionate, alive, and loving
- Decide whom you want to be closer to
- Determine the risks of coming out to certain people

In the next exercise, you'll write about all the people with whom you want to share your sexual orientation. At this point, don't feel you have to follow through with everyone you list. You're not making any promises. The idea is to get you thinking more seriously about how important this is to you.

List all of the names of people you want to come out to.

Family members:

_____

_____

_____

Friends:

_____

_____

_____

Acquaintances:

_____

_____

_____

Work/school colleagues:

_____

_____

_____

For each person, answer the following questions. (You may need to use some extra paper, depending on how many names are included in your list.)

Whom, at this time in your life, do you most want to tell about your sexual orientation?

_____

What are your reasons for coming out to this person now?

_____

_____

_____

_____

What, if anything, do you expect or want to happen by coming out to this person?

_____

_____

_____

_____

What are the risks of coming out to this person?

_____

_____

_____

_____

Do the benefits of coming out to this person outweigh the risks you listed, or do the risks outweigh the benefits?

_____

_____

_____

_____

You may find it helpful to keep the pages on which you've written your analyses of whom you want to tell. Your choices of whom to come out to and what you say may change over the years. For example, Jeremy decided not to tell his grandmother that he was gay, but after hearing her talk openly about her friend's nephew who came out, he realized he wanted her to know.

What Do You Want to Say?

Okay, so you've decided that you want to come out to someone. You've thought about the risks and decided it's the right thing for you to do, or maybe you've decided it's important enough to do it whether the person accepts you or not. What will you actually say when you want to share something this important about yourself? There's always the familiar intro, "I've got something I want to talk to you about." But what do you say next? How do you talk openly about your sexual orientation to someone for the first time? This can be complicated in some situations; at other times, it will be fairly simple and straightforward. No matter how you slice it, you will somehow find the words to express that you are gay, bisexual, or questioning.

What you say and how you say it—whether it's "I'm gay," "I'm bisexual," "I'm in transition," or whatever else you want to express—will be based on a number of factors. It will depend on how you feel about the person you're telling (Is it a friend you are attracted to? Someone you are scared of?); the power the person holds in your life (Is it your boss? A parent on whom you're financially dependent?); and how close your relationship with that person is (Is it a close friend? A colleague? A distant relative?).

Think about the following as you consider what you will say to the person you are coming out to:

- Remember that the person is important to you, otherwise you wouldn't care enough to share who you are.

- Say what you want to say, not what you think the other person wants to hear.

- Finding the right words will become easier the more you practice.

- It's okay to have a little stage fright each time you come out. Do something to relax yourself before you talk about it; for example, take some deep breaths or visualize it going well.

- There is no one right way to say "I'm gay" or "I'm bisexual"— you have to use words that suit your relationship with the person and match the level of heart you want to put into the relationship.

- Don't beat around the bush; be straightforward.

- Think carefully about what you say and speak from your heart.

- Be compassionate.

- If you are angry, don't take your anger out on the other person.

- Take your time to find the right words, but not too much time (don't overanalyze).

- If you can help it, don't make a bigger deal about coming out than you need to. Others will often mirror your reactions to the situation. If you are calm, they will be less apt to be agitated or tense. If you are confident, they will have more confidence in you.

- Practice—by role-playing with a friend, by writing your words down, or by talking to yourself in the mirror.

Choosing Your Words

Be cautious in choosing your words: You may be bursting at the seams to talk about being GBQ, but the person you're telling may be totally confused. Keep in mind that your listener will be dealing with his or her own feelings—maybe strong feelings. If this is something you've kept to yourself for a long time, you will be much more emotional than the other person. You also have a jump on the person: you've already thought about what you're saying while he or she is just now learning about the GBQ part of you.

So what do you say? And how do you go about saying it? Let's break it down. How close are you to the person you're telling? If you're close to the person, it might help to begin by letting him or her know that you've given this a lot of thought or how important he or she is to you. You might also want to explain why you've decided to come out at this point so that the person might better understand your situation. After coming out, you might say, "Do you want to ask me anything about it?" in order to give the person an opportunity to be open without feeling uncomfortable.

The more straightforward you are, the easier it will be on you. Try out some statements you can say when you come out to a close person. Write down the ones you like.

_____

_____

_____

_____

_____

_____

For people not as close to you, perhaps a co-worker or schoolmate, you may want to choose a matter-of-fact, "no room for questions" style. One way to do this is to gracefully embed your coming out in day-to-day discussions. For instance, "When I was at this gay fund-raiser over the weekend . . ." In some situations, however, this way may not communicate what you want; the person may not hear that you're saying that you are GBQ. To be more straightforward, you might share something personal, again embedded in a casual conversation. For example, "My boyfriend and I are thinking of going to the company dinner. Are you going?"

Another approach is to begin a statement with "As a gay/bisexual man, I feel that . . ." A colleague and friend of mine used this as a way to introduce one of his professional talks, and I have found it helpful to use in many professional or new settings because it doesn't require the other person to respond.

Again, try out some coming-out statements and write down the ones you like. This time your statements should be directed to an acquaintance, colleague, or distant relative.

_____

_____

_____

_____

_____

_____

Helpful Hints

- Ask another gay or bisexual person for advice (if you don't feel comfortable asking someone you know, check out the gay/bi chat rooms on the Internet).

- Role-play with someone safe—a friend, another gay or bisexual person, or a therapist—so you can practice what you want to say.

- For coming out to people who live far away from you, write a letter and then follow up with a phone call.

When Should You Do It?

Deciding when you want to come out can be complicated. You may decide to wait, but it may happen that you do it impulsively, because suddenly it feels right. Or you may find yourself obsessing over the decision—analyzing it over and over again and losing sleep over how, or if, you should come out to your brother or colleague or friend. I call this latter situation the *intuitive nudge*; it lets you know that it's time to talk about something, but you're scared. You've probably heard the saying, "The best laid plans go oft astray"; yet, by thinking ahead about when to come out to someone, you are putting yourself in charge. Your timing may not be perfect and you may end up feeling awkward and embarrassed, but the planning you've done will have helped you act calm and collected. No matter what happens, keep in mind that life will go on, and the quicker you move on from a less-than-graceful incident, the more likely it will come out the way you want next time.

Here's what happened to Ian when he came out to his family: "I had it all planned out, how I was going to tell my sisters and my mom and dad. But I kept chickening out. Days and days, and lots of "right" moments, passed by in a blur of mental tugs-of-war. 'Tell them now!... No, now is *not* a good time.' Then, over Thanksgiving dinner, I was stressed by the holidays and my uncle asked me what 'cute young gal' I was dating now. As I passed the turkey, in repressed frustration and excitement, I blurted out, 'I met a man and I'm in love!' Right there in front of Mom, Dad, assorted relatives, and my eighty-year-old grandpa. I was so upset the next morning, I vomited. I did it though, and, you know, it felt so good to get it over with." Ian decided he would not beat himself up over how he handled it, instead he'd learn from it. He also made himself available to answer any questions his family had.

Deciding When to Tell

This exercise is to get you thinking and considering possibilities, not to create any rules for yourself. Your priorities about when to come out will depend on your developmental life cycle (entering college, getting divorced, changing jobs, retiring). This decision will also depend on other circumstances, such as your health, cultural mores, or values about closeness in your relationships. And, of course, like everything else, your priorities will change along with your goals and life structure. In working through this part of the chapter, it may help to go back and review the section about your life plan, in chapter 2.

Person	Now	Soon	Within a year	Whenever

Person	Deadline

For those in the Now or Soon category, set a deadline for yourself. It could be an exact date, an event, etc.:

Helpful Hints

- Talk to someone when you have that person's full attention.
- Find a quiet place or private moment that feels right to you.
- Don't tell someone who is already upset about something—wait for a more appropriate time if you can.
- Keep it simple—tell one person at a time instead of a large group of people who will each react differently.
- Have a supportive person be "on call" to talk to.
- It's okay if you're a little nervous or if your voice or hands are shaky: it happens to the best of us.

Learning from Others

You can learn a lot by observing other GBQ people and asking them about their experiences with coming out. I have had a lot of practice over the years telling people that I am gay. For me, it was helpful to listen to various gay and bisexual friends and clients who have come out to others.

Name a person (or people) in your life who has had coming-out experiences you can ask about and learn from.

_____

_____

_____

The decisions you have to make about coming out are ultimately your own. Exploring the issues and paying attention to other people's methods can help you to find your own way.

9

Out in Your
Own Right

To understand a given individual's experience as [he] comes to [his] identity, one must first understand that individual; [gay and bisexual] identity formation is an addition to and not a substitute for the developmental process we all pursue.

—Janis Bohan, *Psychology and Sexual Orientation*

Kirk used to feel that he should come out to everybody and that, eventually, he would. He was in the early stages of coming out. Over the course of ten years, he changed this belief, deciding he would be selective about whom he told and when. Kirk now rarely comes out to colleagues. When he does, it's in the course of normal communication about his personal life, and it depends on how close he wants to be to the person he's talking to. He is out to his family of origin, and although it is a problem for some family members, Kirk lets it be their problem, not his. He goes on being who he is and sharing what he feels.

Kirk didn't find his way instantly, and, unfortunately, neither will you. But you've already established a framework for your expectations and you have a good idea of whom you want to tell, what to say, and when. Your task now is to use this information in conjunction with what you've learned about the changing stages of your life. Remember that how and to whom you come out will likely continue to change. You will probably come out numerous times and in numerous ways throughout your entire life. As time passes, your decision process will be more instinctive, and you will learn what works for you and what doesn't.

The Stages of Coming Out

Exploring where you are or want to be in your coming-out process will facilitate your sense of confidence and offer direction as you come out every day. There are several versions of the stages of coming out. Most of them are typical of a gay man's process, but they may also apply to you if you are bisexual or questioning. I'll point out some differences between the stages for bisexual men later in this section.

Defining coming-out stages has considerable value and relevance to many GBQ men in their everyday coming-out process. The emphasis here is not to lock yourself into someone else's definition of a stage, but to guide you in finding your way along the path. In fact, I encourage you to look to these stages only as general guidelines (especially if you are a part of a non-Anglo culture or living in a rural or culturally repressed area). Ultimately, you must construct your own path, molding it from what you read here or creating it anew.

The stages in these models are not necessarily linear. Many people skip around; they do some, then go back and work through others again and again. (Note that these are just a few of the major coming-out stage models. If you are interested in additional studies in this area by other experts in the field, see: Coleman 1982; Savin-Williams and Cohen 1996.)

Vivienne Cass' Stages

One of the originators of the concept of coming out in stages was Vivienne Cass, a clinical psychologist in the department of social inquiry at Murdoch University in Western Australia. Her coming-out model addresses the development of gay identity over the course of six stages. As an example, we'll follow Joe through the Cass stages. As you read, imagine yourself going through the same stages. If you are bisexual, think about how your experience would be different or the same.

1. Confusion. Joe had same-sex feelings in high school, but he dated girls. He had always kept his homosexual feelings to himself. "Am I heterosexual?" "Is this a passing thing?" "Maybe I'm bisexual." These were the questions he asked himself. He had strong, passionate feelings for men and was not in love with any of the women he dated.

2. Comparison. "How am I like the gay people I meet?" Joe began to ask himself. "I feel similar in some ways, yet different in others. And

I think these guys are a real turn-on." In this stage, Joe compared himself to gay and bisexual men he knew about, trying to find his own point of reference.

3. *Tolerance.* "Being gay is okay for me, but it still feels uncomfortable at times."

4. *Acceptance.* Here, Joe says, "I feel really okay about being a gay man. I accept that it is a part of who I am, just like my brown eyes and stout build."

5. *Pride.* This stage reveals more enthusiasm in Joe. He proclaims, "I am proud to be gay and a part of the gay, bisexual, and lesbian community. I want to do some good for it. I'm going to the pride parade and I may even volunteer at the community center."

6. *Synthesis.* This final stage is about uniting your public and private selves into one identity. In it, Joe says, "I am a part of the bigger community I live in. I have some really close heterosexual friends, I'm a softball coach for a youth group, and I'm out to most people. To me being gay is a natural part of who I am as a lover, employee, volunteer, neighbor, and friend."

Now answer the following questions about yourself:

In comparison to Joe, where are you in the stages?

_____

_____

_____

_____

Does this model fit for you or would you change it? How has your path differed from Joe's?

_____

_____

_____

_____

John Grace's Stages

John Grace has written and presented numerous articles about coming out in a homophobic environment. He previously coordinated the first "main stream" program for gay and lesbian counseling in Minneapolis,

Minnesota. In 1992, Grace talked about the following five-stage process of gay development and coming out:

1. Emergence. "I accept my gay/bisexual feelings and I'm gonna go for it."

2. Acknowledgment. "Being gay/bisexual is a respectable and viable way to love someone."

3. Finding community. "I think I'll check out what other gay/bisexual people are doing and find out where I belong in the community."

4. First relationship. "I want to share my life with someone I love. I want to go places and be with people where I am recognized as having an important and valued relationship."

5. Self-definition and reintegration. "I'm looking into the meaning of my life as a gay/bisexual person, and I've got some of the same questions about life and its meaning as everyone else."

Stages for Bisexuals

For bisexuals, the stages of coming out look more like the following, as defined by Weinburg, Williams, and Pryor in 1994:

1. Initial confusion. "Who am I attracted to—men or women? I'm not sure if I consider myself heterosexual, gay, or bisexual."

2. Finding and applying the label "I am bisexual." "Maybe it's okay to be attracted to both sexes to one degree or another. I guess I'm bisexual."

3. Settling into a bisexual identity. "I'm comfortable knowing I'm interested in men and women and that I'm bisexual."

4. Continued uncertainty. "I sometimes feel uncertain about whether I'm gay or heterosexual when I find myself more interested in one sex than the other. Besides, there's not much support for being bisexual in a world of heterosexual and gay people."

The theory behind these stages is that if you are bisexual, there is not yet a well-established framework for validation and support.

In all fairness, bisexuals may feel confused and uncertain at times, but need not become stuck in permanent uncertainty as stage 4 suggests. You may want to keep in mind that bisexual individuals typically come to their identity after an established heterosexual or homosexual identity. On the other hand, some people align themselves with a bisexual identity before settling on the label of heterosexual or gay.

If you identify yourself as bisexual, does this model fit for you? How, in your experience, does your coming-out process compare (at least so far)?

_____

_____

_____

_____

Pamela Rust's Social Constructionist Model

Pamela Rust (1992, 1993) decried the developmental model of coming to terms with one's sexuality and recommended a *social constructionist model* in which gay or bisexual individuals describe themselves according to the social and political context at the time. This approach defines your sexual orientation according to your current social context, rather than being gay or bisexual at your core or essence. The implication of this model is that your sexual orientation is more subject to being shaped by social and cultural influences than by an internal sense of who you are. You therefore would be more subject to the ebb and flow of sociocultural changes and opinions.

Research by Rust and others suggests, especially for bisexuals, that the coming-out process may be oriented more toward tasks than stages. For example, Twining (1983) suggested that bisexual women face the tasks of self-acceptance, resolving societal homophobia, developing a support network, deciding to whom they would disclose, and coping with concerns about coming out professionally. Some of this and other research also suggests bisexuality emerges from both heterosexual- and homosexual-established identity.

How, in your experience, does your identity formation compare with the social constructionist model of describing yourself in relation to your current environment?

_____

_____

_____

_____

I believe there is a middle road to all these stages. Gay, bisexual, or questioning, each man must somehow define his own way. As you come out to yourself and to others and cast aside negative judgments and societal prejudice, you will eventually find some comfortable place that says, "I have arrived and I'm gay/bisexual." Maybe in your coming-out process, you can come to the point of saying, "I'm gay/bisexual but I'm not through experimenting and learning about my sexuality. I don't feel comfortable labeling myself."

Mel fits into this more sexually flexible orientation. He isn't comfortable with a locked-in definition of himself and his sexual orientation or path. Mel lives in San Francisco. He is twenty-eight years old and has been out as a gay man since high school. He has been politically active in gender movements and believes in acceptance of all sexual orientations. He's had long-term relationships with both men and women. After struggling with his sexual identity, experiencing discrimination, and coming to terms with himself as a gay man, he is now rethinking his feelings and exploring his desires for women according to *all* of his needs. He does not want to be restricted from the opportunity to meet and be with women. Rather than classify himself as strictly gay or bisexual at this time in his life, Mel describes himself as a "loving, sexual being with diverse needs." He adds, "Right now this is for me and it's the way I believe people should look at gender and sexuality."

What Is Your Way?

Now that you have some information about different ways of coming out and the stages that people go through, what do you think of your own coming-out process? What is your way? Again, take some time with this. Walk with these ideas and look at where you are in your life structure. Try to express what you really want as a GBQ man at this time in your life.

Write about what you want in terms of coming out—now, in the future, and every day. Describe what you see as your upcoming challenges in this area. You may want to use as a framework one of the coming-out models discussed, or you can formulate your own.

For his response to this exercise, Isaac wrote: "I think the hardest thing for me in coming out in my own way is to be honest to my family, because they are very religious and nasty about sin and morals and all that. I may want to limit my contact with them for a while. I also want to give myself permission to come out to people at work when I'm good and ready, and not pressure myself one way or the other. With my close friends, I think I want to keep speaking my truth about my sexual and love feelings. And I want to stand up to those who speak out against gays and bisexuals."

What is your way of coming out?

_____

_____

_____

_____

_____

Coping Tools and Strategies

Coming out over time will require that you use a variety of coping skills. You need to find the ones that work best for you. Coming out to others and accepting yourself as a GBQ man is the ultimate example of an emotional challenge. During your individual coming-out process you will be helped by balancing your feelings with thoughtful decision making. Use the easy-to-think-about coping tools and self-talk strategies in this section to get you through the tough times. Try to acknowledge and feel your pain, rather than self-medicating with drugs, alcohol, food, or sex. Avoid isolating yourself from others. These are negative coping styles that do not resolve your issues but instead can cause additional problems. These strategies offer real help with the formidable task of being real and dealing with the prejudice that gay and bisexual people face.

Be aware that disclosing your sexual orientation is a positive act. Telling others you are GBQ gives you a greater sense of freedom and increases the possibility for genuine acceptance and inner satisfaction. Research suggests that, in the long run, coming out to others is associated with a positive sense of well-being.

Learn from adversity. Being GBQ may have brought difficult and hurtful experiences to you, including discrimination and prejudice. You can grow stronger from your experiences—something that might not have happened if life had been easier. Use it to your advantage.

Be patient; stay encouraged. When you come out to others, you must be willing to accept that you won't always get the results you want. Patience—with yourself as well as others—will serve you well. Parents, peers, and the other people in your life often take a while to "come around" and accept you for who you are. Being patient with your coming-out process also means giving yourself time to tell people in your own way and in your own time. Work toward staying positive, despite the shock reactions or rejection you may encounter.

Be aware that others will have their own pace for acceptance. Tolerance is usually followed by acceptance. Everyone you tell will have his or her own way of dealing with it.

Try to understand the point of view of the person you're telling. Remember—although *you've* been living with this for a long time, the person you're telling doesn't live inside you and won't ever really know what it's like for you.

Trust your instincts. Come out when it feels right. If you truly think you should wait, trust that instinct.

Remember to speak your truth. Your truth is about you as a GBQ man. When you tell others about yourself, do it from your heart, in a way that feels real, honest, thoughtful, and emotionally genuine.

Stretch yourself to tell the truth. Don't fake it, if you can help it. Make a commitment to share who you are as a GBQ man—even when the situation could be hard or uncomfortable.

*Stop and think about what you really want; **then** share it.* It pays to think about whom to tell, how to say it, and when you want to come out. Don't just blurt it out.

Listen to others' opinions, unless they're mean, harmful, cruel, or disrespectful. If you listen to *their* feelings about your being gay or bisexual, people will be more willing to listen to *you* and to hear about who you are as a GBQ man. On the other hand, if someone's being disrespectful or cruel, you owe it to yourself to tell the person that you want him or her to behave in a different way. Say that you will continue talking and listening only when he or she is being respectful.

Ask yourself, "Why do I need to come out to this person?" Is it for your benefit or for the person's? Do you truly care about this person enough to let him or her in? Do you simply need to make a political statement? Are you trying to be more comfortable with who you are?

Use your positive coming-out experiences as an anchor. Think about and remember all the positive coming-out experiences you have had. They'll help give you continued strength to come out.

Trust that it will get easier and more natural. Coming out may be difficult and challenging when you meet yet another stranger and have to decide whether to come out or not as you get to know him or her. But it does seem to become easier and to feel more natural as time goes on.

Just When You Thought It Was Over . . .

Part of coming out every day means being ready for occasional adversity. Sometimes, when you have finally settled into feeling okay about your sexual orientation and can easily share that you have a crush on the man next door or that your partner is a guy, along comes trouble: some homophobic jerk happens into your path, or up crops an old fear of rejection that makes you want to eat a half-gallon of Jamoca Almond Fudge ice cream.

Andrew, a well-adjusted, twenty-five-year-old gay man, had been out for a good while. He was active in the community center and enjoyed his participation in the local gay men's choir. He had been comfortable for many years choosing whom and when to tell that he was gay. He started seeing a man who was not yet out and was uncomfortable socializing with Andrew's gay friends and even being seen with Andrew. Around the same time, Andrew's brother decided to tell him how uneasy he was with Andrew's homosexuality and asked him not to bring his lover to family affairs. Andrew had become pretty snug in his own skin; now, he once again had to face issues associated with coming out. He also had to deal with his brother's reluctance and homophobia. For Andrew this brought up old feelings of shame, anger at the judgments of others, and frustration about the energy it took to be understanding and patient with his new boyfriend. After all, he was comfortable with his sexuality. Why should he have to deal with someone else's conflicts or lack of development at this stage in the game? Andrew was disappointed in himself and his confidence was shaken.

Facing the ups and downs of being gay and out is part of the program for all of us. Homophobia doesn't ever seem to go away, no matter how many understanding and evolved people we associate with. And sometimes it will require all your energy to deal with it. This is a fact of gay or bisexual existence, and it can be even harder when you are stressed or are dealing with other life issues. As long as you live in a world of diverse people with strong beliefs and prejudices, you will at least sometimes have to face society's insecurities with bisexuality and homosexuality. A few of your own old lingering hurts and doubts are bound to hang around, too.

Acknowledging and welcoming your individuality may always be challenging. So it's a wise man who accepts that there will always be some form of prejudice in the world. I'm not saying you should accept prejudice, hate, and disrespect toward you as a GBQ man, nor that you should accept that you can't do anything about it. Just accept that it exists. Continue to be your best; keep on being genuine and true to yourself as a GBQ man, and you will almost always reap the benefits of serenity and mental happiness.

What are a few things you can do to support yourself during the stress of coming out? How can you cope with prejudice?

_____

_____

_____

_____

_____

_____

A Letter of Pride

Coming out is a process. This exercise is aimed at helping you establish a marker as to where you are in the process. When you're done you'll not only be able to pinpoint where you are now, but you'll be able to appreciate how far you've come.

Write a letter to yourself using the following suggestions:

- Tell yourself how proud you are to be a GBQ man.

- Acknowledge your courage for being true to yourself.

- Point out where you think you are in the coming-out process. Describe how it feels.

- Give yourself a few pointers about how to get through the hard times when others are critical or judgmental of your life as a GBQ man.

- Say some supportive things to help you when your confidence is wavering or you're having doubts.

When you're finished with your letter, mail it! Actually put a stamp on it and mail it. When it's delivered, save it (opened or unopened) in a special place that you won't forget. When you need it most, it'll be there to read and offer support from your most enthusiastic fan: yourself.

10

Family Ties

Intimacy requires courage because risk is inescapable.
We cannot know at the onset how the relationship will affect us.

—Rollo May, *The Courage to Create*

So, here you are coming out every day and you realize, "Oops, I forgot to tell my parents." Many GBQ men are virtually paralyzed by the thought of telling their folks. If your parents are in your life in some way and you have already told them, great—be proud of this immense accomplishment and make use of their support as much as you see fit. If you haven't come out to your parents yet, that's okay. It's a tough decision to make, and harder still to carry out.

Coming out to parents and others is one part of becoming closer to the people in your life; honest, intimate relationships begin here. In chapter 8, you worked on analyzing the very important decision of whether to come out and to whom. If you are still in the process of building solid, meaningful relationships and narrowing the field of "those who don't know," then you are part of a large community of GBQ men.

This chapter takes you another step in the process of being out. It's about taking risks and deepening your relationships with your family of origin. Coming out to a family member is a personal decision and should always be up to you. It's also quite challenging and calls for you to gather your supports around you. When all is said and done, though, you will achieve more intimacy with certain family members than you ever imagined possible; you may also find that some members of your family are not yet ready to accept you as a GBQ man.

What You Gain from Honest Family Relationships

Here are some benefits you may get from being out to your family:

- Relief—from the pressure of keeping a secret

- Inner strength and confidence

- Greater self-acceptance

- Freedom to show your vacation photos without having to pretend he's your tour guide

- Freedom to talk about what really matters to you

- Desire to listen to what really matters to others

- Freedom to mention your lover's/partner's name

- Freedom to take your lover/partner to family events

- Freedom to use the word *gay* or *bisexual* without wincing

Can you think of some others?

- _____

- _____

- _____

- _____

Including Your Family of Origin in Your Lifelong Coming-Out Process

This section will help you hone in on the family members you want to come out to and look at ways you can help them as you come out.

First, who knows and who doesn't? In the following table, make a list of family members who know and don't know that you're GBQ. Check the appropriate column to indicate whether you're out to the person or not, or you're out but you want to be able to talk to him or her more openly about it.

Family Member	Not Out	Out	Out, But Not Open
Mother			
Father			
Brother			
Sister			
Grandmother			
Grandfather			
Cousin			
Uncle			
Aunt			

For the people you haven't told yet or the ones to whom you don't talk much about your sexuality, what would it mean for you to tell them? What would it mean if you tried to get closer and be more open? Why is it important to you? How will it bring you closer to the person, and how will it benefit you to talk to this person about your life, loves, and interests as a GBQ man? Another way to think about it is, what do you have to gain and what do you lose by having this person really get to know you? Here's an example: "Mom and I are as not as close as we

Family Member	Why It's Important to Get Closer
_____	_____
	_____
	_____
_____	_____
	_____
	_____
	_____
	_____
_____	_____
	_____
	_____
_____	_____
	_____
	_____
_____	_____
	_____
	_____
_____	_____
	_____
	_____
_____	_____
	_____
	_____
_____	_____
	_____
	_____
_____	_____
	_____
	_____

used to be—I miss sharing with her stuff that is meaningful and interesting." "But I might want to prepare myself for some silence—Mom sometimes pulls away and seems cold when hit with emotional issues." Think about how being honest about yourself with specific family members may have helped to develop your relationship with them. How did it work out in the past? Might it be something to work on in the future?

If you have more to say about it than the table will hold, continue writing about this in your journal or in the extra space provided:

_____

_____

_____

_____

_____

_____

Help Your Family Members along the Way

You may be like a lot of men who have never mentioned the G(ay) word or the B(isexual) word to their family members. You may find that using the actual words will break through barriers. Your sexual orientation may still be something your family needs time to assimilate and live with for a while. You can also facilitate their process if you choose. How do you feel about helping certain family members with their coming-to-terms process?

Keep in mind that you and your family's emotions may lead to a loss of perspective. You can help yourself by remembering that your family is new to what you're telling them. Even if they have suspected you are GBQ, hearing it makes it real. And no matter how open-minded they are, it might make them uncomfortable. Try putting yourself in their shoes to understand why they feel the way they do; empathy is truly one of the keys to better communication. As you try to understand their point of view, try to help them understand yours. Simply put: people are more willing to listen to you if you listen to them. Of course, this doesn't mean you have to agree with them, nor does it guarantee your sexual orientation will be accepted. However, experience shows that empathy improves intimacy.

Maybe one of your family members is "limping along" a bit on the path to a healthy relationship with you as a GBQ man. If you want that person to walk beside you, here are some suggestions that may help:

- Ask the person to write out a list of questions for you—things he or she has been wondering about your life and about being GBQ.

- Get the person a book about the subject, such as *Beyond Acceptance* (see resources section).

- Give the person a newsletter or brochure from PFLAG (Parents and Friends of Lesbians and Gays), or tell him or her about a PFLAG meeting going on in your community (see resources section).

- Turn the person on to some gay- or bisexual-positive plays, documentaries, or movies that have realistic gay or bisexual characters (no, not the porno ones).

- Sit down with the person for a heart-to-heart conversation over coffee in a private, neutral place.

- Decide how much you want to share with the person. Keep your boundaries appropriate—skip the nitty-gritty details.

- Acknowledge the smallest steps made towards acceptance and tell the person how much you appreciate the effort.

Try to avoid pushing too much. Pay attention to your timing—is the person too stressed or caught up in his or her own emotions to be open to a heart-to-heart? If you attempt a heart-to-heart discussion and it's a flop, don't fret—try another time when the other person has had a chance to chew on your newfound intimacy and digest it a bit. Also, remember that you don't have to defend yourself if people get angry at you—let it be their "stuff"; try to be open and listen without subjecting yourself to disrespect or hurtful tirades.

Don't do what Larry did: While visiting his family for Thanksgiving, he decided to have one of those heart-to hearts with his parents over a 1:00 A.M. nightcap after a long, stressful day. Can't blame a guy for trying though—his heart was in the right place, but his timing and delivery left something to be desired. Larry's parents had also decided to finally confront their feelings and ask all the questions they had about his sexuality. Larry could only sigh as they launched into a harangue telling him how to live his life and at one point he lost his composure and yelled, "I'll do what I damn well please, I'm an adult!" Over coffee the next morning, Larry took the first step to apologize for his part of the drama and they all agreed to try to discuss their feelings more calmly.

Are You Sure You Want to Tell?

You may not care at all about creating a closer relationship with some family members. It may not be important to you to include them in your innermost personal GBQ life. Or you may have decided not to share with someone who is violent, has total financial control over your life, or has an active substance-abuse problem.

But maybe there's a member of your family from whom you are separated or estranged by tension or misunderstanding about your being GBQ. You may want to consider how it might be for you to change your relationship with this person, and share the GBQ parts of your life. Consider the possibilities. Do a thoughtful evaluation of the pros and cons of being more intimate with this person. Take the time to consider the effects of being open and being close.

The issues may be different when coming out to different family members. For example, parents may see your sexual orientation as due to something they did wrong in raising you. A father may see your sexuality as a threat to his masculinity or to how close he can be with you. While your mother may blame herself for being overprotective of you. Just as parents' reactions do, siblings' reactions depend on how close they feel to you and the possible influence they've had on you. Their reactions also depend on their birth order and how identified they are with you. Aunts, uncles, grandparents, and others' reactions will depend on how close they are to you and the general nature of your past and current relationship. All family members' reactions are heavily weighted by their expectations of you, attitudes towards homosexuality, and shame about what other's will think. Of course, the acceptance you receive from different family members can range from complete rejection to complete acceptance. Fortunately, the former is rare.

Is there is someone in your family who doesn't yet know about your sexuality, or who is uncomfortable with what they know? Are you unsure about sharing your gay or bisexual orientation? If you have serious doubts, what are they? Consider the pros and cons and write about them here.

Taking the Leap into Closeness: A Family Story

Carl is twenty-two and gay. He has never been very close to his mother, but has always been able to talk to his father and next oldest brother about anything. Carl was sure that his parents knew he was gay, but he'd never talked about it with them. He was afraid that really talking openly about the aspects of his gay life would blow what little relationship he had with his mother and damage the intimacy he felt with his brother and father. In studying his feelings, Carl realized that it was not just fear of rejection or loss that was holding him back, but his own homophobia and fear of how he would be judged. Carl tended to get down on himself for being "different" and "less manly." He reminded himself that getting the improved intimacy he wanted was more important than pride or fear and he took the risk. It took a year for his brother to accept Carl's sexuality, and his father was more loving than before. The situation with his mother actually improved: she ended up inviting Carl and his lover for the next holiday gathering.

Stages of Family Acceptance

You've already read a lot about phases, stages, and transitions in this book. In terms of your family's acceptance of your coming out, some universal patterns and stages have come to light. I've added some additional categories, based on my own clinical and personal experiences, that I have found to be relevant.

To a certain degree, the stages of family acceptance parallel the stages experienced after the loss of a loved one (Kubler-Ross 1969; Savin-Williams 1996). That's because the family's old views of you may have died, and you are not (in some ways) who you used to be. Like all such stage models, the ones described here are common patterns—they're not set in stone. Nor do they occur in a particular sequence. People may even repeat some stages. In other words, bear in mind the same caution mentioned in earlier chapters: Use these stages as guidelines to prepare yourself for how others may potentially react. Don't make these stages into rules. Remember, also, that all family members won't move in unison. One parent may be at one stage, while another is moving ahead or following behind.

Ryan's Family

As an example, let's begin by getting to know Ryan and his family and then follow them through their stages of acceptance. At thirty-three, Ryan decided to finally tell his parents and siblings he was gay. When Ryan was growing up, the family had lived in a distant rural community. Ryan now lives in Boston, his brother works in a town close to his parents, and his sister lives in a large city on the West Coast. Ryan doesn't feel as close to his sister since she got married and started a family, but still talks to his brother regularly. He calls his parents on weekends and keeps their conversations superficial. He decided to write letters to his parents, brother, and sister, starting each one out with "I know I'm a gay man, but I have been scared to tell you. There's no one special in my life yet, and I'm healthy." He went on to tell each of them that he wanted to be closer to them, even if it was hard for them to accept his sexuality.

The Stages

Denial or confusion. Ryan's father thought, "No way, he can't be, not my Ryan—he's not one of those sissy boys." His mother felt it was "just a phase" and he'd be over it soon enough. His brother and sister talked to each other: "I always wondered, but I'm confused—he dated all those girls and seemed so interested in them."

Anger or guilt. Ryan's father said to him, "I wish I hadn't told you to quit football—I didn't push you enough to be competitive." His mother said, "Maybe I mothered him too much." His sister defiantly disapproved, "You only think of yourself, Ryan—look how you're upsetting Mom and Dad." She stayed stuck in this process longer then the rest of her family.

Bargaining. Ryan's brother told him, "You haven't tried to be with girls enough—if you try, you can kick this thing." His father tried to remind him, "You'll get over this."

Depression and fear. Ryan's mother told him, "I don't know if I can take this. It scares me to think what your life will be like as a gay man." His father said, "I can't believe this is happening to our family."

Tolerance. Ryan's mother was forthright: "I'm embarrassed to tell anybody anything about you, because they might figure out you're gay." His brother said, "I can deal with you being different, even liking men, but don't talk about it so much."

Acceptance. "All right, I can accept that you are gay—go ahead and introduce me to your friends. I want to know you and who you are more completely," his father smiled.

Now answer the following questions about your own family.

In terms of these stages of acceptance, where do your family members fit?

_____

_____

_____

_____

How do various members of your family differ from one another in their levels of acceptance?

_____

_____

_____

_____

How do these levels of acceptance affect you (how you feel, how you think about things, and how you act)?

_____

_____

_____

By understanding the "acceptance stage" a family member is in, you can position yourself to

- Be more empathic with certain family members

- Clarify what you want to do in response to denial, guilt, or other negative emotions

- Feel better by examining and understanding your feelings and thoughts about the other person's reactions

- Help them, if you want, to understand they are not alone by offering to share information about resources, like PFLAG, books, and support groups

Here Today, Out Tomorrow

Your destiny lies before you. Build family relationships that support your love for your family, your values, and the closeness you desire. As you come out to various family members, it's likely that you will strengthen your relationships with them; unfortunately, others may grow distant, while a few will move out of your life completely.

You may end up mourning the loss of a relationship or two, but in the long run, your relationships with family will no longer require you to be secretive or guarded. Instead your relationships will be open, honest, and meaningful.

11

Finding Friends
and Lovers

*Friendship multiplies the good of life and divides the evil. 'Tis the
sole remedy against misfortune, the very ventilation of the soul.*

—Baltasar Gracián,
The Art of Worldly Wisdom

In this chapter, you can take some time to explore how to add to and
create your own community of friends, lovers, and companions and how
to find the relationships you want. You'll also look at countering unhealthy dependencies that you may have developed in some of your past
and present relationships.

What You Gain from Honest
Relationships

There is nothing that can compare, nothing more rewarding, than estab-
lishing a long-term love relationship and solid friendships to heal the
shame and pain of rejection—someone to walk through the tough times
with; someone to help you celebrate the pride and power of being out;
someone who gives you support and affection and helps you be unique,
strong, and passionate as a GBQ man.

Here are some benefits you may get from being out to your friends, peers, and colleagues:

- Relief—from the pressure of keeping a secret
- Inner strength and confidence
- True intimacy
- Greater self-acceptance
- Freedom to talk about what really matters to you
- Desire to listen to what really matters to others
- More passion in your love relationships
- Freedom to talk about guys you find attractive
- Freedom to mention your lover's/partner's name

A Self-Survey

Answer the questions in this self-survey to help define what you're looking for in your relationships. Think about what you want and need from friends, community members, co-workers, and lovers. Your goal here is to figure out what you want and need. This survey will help you think about and set some relationship goals and will set you on track to achieve your goals.

Friends

Friends are your most valuable resource. They can be a precious source of strength, support, purpose, and love. As a GBQ man, a friend can be your lifeline to celebration, hugs, and words of wisdom, taking the edge off unwanted loneliness and offering you moments of comfort and healing.

As an out GBQ man, what do you want in a friend at this time in your life?

_____

_____

_____

_____

Do you specifically want some friends who are of a certain race, culture, religious background, or sexual orientation? In what way are these qualities important to you as a GBQ man?

_____

_____

_____

_____

As an out GBQ man, what do you want from your heterosexual friends?

_____

_____

_____

How have you found friends in the past and how can you use what you already know to improve upon your friend-finding abilities?

_____

_____

_____

How is it different for you to find friends as an out GBQ man?

_____

_____

_____

List two ways you think you can be more proactive _now_, to meet the kinds of friends you want in your current life.

_____

_____

_____

_____

Community

Recall what a sense of community means to you. What does having a community feel like? What is it like to embrace and be embraced by your ideal community? Community can provide you with a sense of belonging; it can be made up of the sights and sounds, warmth and affections of the GBQ men you have to dinner; it can include the men and women you share coffee with or attend movies, concerts, or plays with; your neighbor, your classmates, your fellow colleagues, your spiritual cohorts. On a larger scale, your community may be represented by a part of the city you live in, a cultural region, or the peoples of your heritage. Community is both large and small and what you make it. By creating your own community of people who respect your authenticity as a GBQ man, you provide yourself with an elixir of hope, belonging, and pride.

What are you looking for in a community? Include any ethnic, cultural, gender, and sexual orientation preferences.

_____

_____

_____

_____

In terms of creating a community, how is it different for you now, as a GBQ man, from when you were not open (to yourself or others) about your sexuality?

_____

_____

_____

_____

List two ways you think you can be more proactive *now*, to meet the kind of people and form the community you want in your current life.

_____

_____

_____

_____

Sex and Love Relationships

We'll do a lot more work on this subject in the upcoming section. For now, for the purpose of this self-survey, define what you want in a romantic relationship.

What kind of person do I want to be with? (Physical characteristics, personality, intelligence, career, income, interests)

_____

_____

What kind of romantic relationship do I want to have? (Dating, short-term, commitment, monogamous versus open, live-in, marriage)

_____

_____

_____

_____

What are your long-term goals for a relationship?

_____

_____

_____

_____

Your Lover: Knowing Who and What You Want

So you want to meet the man of your dreams—"Fabio, the wonderful," as one of my friends calls his perfect yet undiscovered mate. "He's The One, I am sure of it," I've heard another friend say for the umpteenth time—only to be dumped a week later by Mr. Right. "Do you really know what you want," I sarcastically ribbed, "or do you like emotionally unavailable men?" I've known many men who are bright, handsome, and have a solid career, yet they still can't seem to meet the person who is right for them. Sometimes people's expectations of relationships are too high—they may even mirror the unfulfilled parts of themselves they are trying to capture or are the results of the wreckage perfectionism creates. Not to be too much of a fatalist here, but unless you get out of your own way psychologically (that is, stop sabotaging the way you choose and meet potential intimate partners) and become clear on who and what you want, you may be setting yourself up to dance the same dance by continuing to pursue frustrating relationships.

Many people think they know what they want, but when they get down to it, they're as vague on this important concept as they are about what to have for dinner tonight. Not knowing makes it harder to see it when it walks by. Some make the mistake of thinking they have to be handsome, drive a nice car, or have a stunning career or huge trust fund in order to be attractive to potential companions. Sure—if you have some of that stuff it may not hurt, but it's really just icing on the cake.

What Kind of Person Do You Want?

You drive up to a fast-food restaurant and the speaker clown says "Can I help you?" You say, "I want something to eat."

The clown says, "Sir, what might you like?" You stare back blankly. "Something fried and something with meat."

"Can you be more specific?"

"Yeah, give me a hamburger."

"What do you want on your hamburger?" the clown says impatiently.

Coming out of your daze, you answer, "Oh, pickles, catsup, and cheese please."

If you know what you want, you're more likely to get it. Of course, the other, inflexible extreme is having every characteristic of your ideal person planned out in minute detail, down to where the person buys clothes or was raised.

Do you think you need to be any more specific about the kind of person you're looking for than you were in the previous section? If so, you can add to the characteristics you are looking for in this section. It may help to think about the type of person that you really enjoy talking to and having fun with, looking at, and cuddling with.

_____

_____

_____

_____

What Kind of Relationship Do You Want?

The next two sections are designed to launch you more successfully on your quest for the relationship you want. If you already have the relationship you want, you might read through these sections to add to your awareness any wants you haven't yet considered. These exercises are meant to precisely pinpoint what you feel, think, and aspire to in passion and love.

First, before you go shopping for the man (or woman) you want, prioritize the kind of a relationship you want. Here's a checklist to help you out; you can add items to it and number them to prioritize as needed.

What is important to me in finding and having a relationship at this time in my life?

_____ I don't want to have to make too many changes.

_____ I want to meet some new friends before I start dating.

_____ I need to date a lot of different people.

_____ I'm ready to date a few "quality" people who might be real candidates for a relationship.

_____ I want to be sexual without any commitments.

_____ I'm ready to meet someone with whom I can settle down.

_____ I want an exclusive, monogamous relationship.

_____ I want to be "married" and to go through a ceremony to affirm love and commitment.

_____ I want to have children in the relationship.

_____ I want a committed relationship that's "open," where I can be sexual with other people.

_____ I want to change my current relationship to be monogamous.

_____ I want to change my current relationship to be nonmonogamous.

_____ I have no idea at all what I want.

_____ I'm not ready to commit to what I want.

_____ _____

_____ _____

_____ _____

If your long-term goals for a relationship are different from some of the goals you just identified, put a star by those items.

Looking back at what you just did, how do these wants mesh with or interfere with the type of relationship you are currently in or the people you've been dating or courting. How do you want to change your situation to better meet your goals?

_____

_____

_____

_____

Naming the One You Love

Gay and bisexual people have had to borrow names from heterosexual unions and sometimes create their own names for erotic and love relationships. The issue of what to call one another also comes up when you meet people and are deciding how out you want to be about your sexuality and whether you want to out the both of you. Some of the names are rather blatantly descriptive, some are more true to how you feel about one another, and some are only useful until you find something that really fits for you. Circle the ones you like. What's the difference for you?

Lover	Companion	Boyfriend/girlfriend
Sleeping buddy	Husband/wife	Sex pal
Partner	Intimate other	Significant other
My friend		

Your ideas for names:

_____

_____

Suggestions from the Battlefield

A colleague and I led gay men's groups for several years. Of course, a favorite topic in these groups was how to find the man they wanted to love. Here are some suggestions gathered as a result of these discussions and from my own clinical experience working with gay and bisexual men. These suggestions have proven helpful in getting people what they want in relationships.

- Be genuine. Don't try to be someone you're not.

- Don't resist rejection. It's better to be rejected early on than later when you have more of yourself invested.

- Remember that you can't make someone love you.

- Taking care of yourself—your body, health, mind, finances, home— is attractive.

- Being full of yourself is not attractive.

- Listen, ask caring questions, listen, share about yourself, and then listen some more.

- Resist hopping into bed on the first date.

- Try not to take yourself too seriously; laugh at your mistakes and have some fun.

- Recognize your own homophobia when it comes up and work on changing it.

- Nice things do sometimes come in pretty packages, but looks can be deceiving.

- It is a person's mind and heart that will sustain a relationship.

- You cannot change someone into what you want.

- Take risks to meet new people.

- Your friends are your best resource for meeting potential partners.

- The personals are a legitimate resource to meet a gay or bisexual companion. Be careful, give it time, and meet in a neutral spot first.

- Know what you want and be proactive about getting it.

Develop Your Personal Ritual to Help You Get What You Want

This story is a personal one and very sacred for me: I have a close friend and colleague with whom I've created a tradition. We go away to a secluded Zen retreat once each summer. Many years ago, we took a hike along the river there and waded deep into its pools. We'd decided we wanted to do a "man-finding ritual" since we weren't having any luck meeting and dating men who were "our type." This was a serious but fun ritual. We found various items in and around the river (a penny, a feather, bark, rocks, and so on) that represented who we wanted. We shared and talked with each other about what we really wanted in a man. Then we arranged our treasures into a small nature sculpture, meditated on the visions of our hoped-for guys, and cast our desires out to the universe.

No, this was not witchcraft, but rather a deep soul-searching exercise. This event helped me to get clear on what I wanted, and I came away from the experience able to let go of my obsession with meeting Mr. Right. Call it serendipity, but three months later my friend and his newfound partner introduced me to the man with whom I've shared my life ever since. This experience had a significant impact on my belief that by clarifying my desires and using a ritual to deepen my processes, I am more able to get what I want.

Now it's your turn. Create your own ritual to meet the kind of person you want now. Here are some ideas: Visualize your person. Create a piece of art to represent your wants. Write a list of all the things you desire in a person and place it outside in your garden or in the woods somewhere. In your journal, create a running dialogue between yourself and your envisioned partner. Light some incense, create a special altar with symbolic objects, and meditate on an image of the person you want.

What is your ritual for knowing and getting what you want?

_____

_____

Codependency and Counterdependency

You may find yourself getting stuck in patterns where you give away too much of your independence in relationships. You may be aware that your self-esteem plummets, you put others' needs before your own, and/or you lose a sense of what is right for you and what you want when you pair up with someone. These are all potential symptoms of *codependency*.

On the other hand, you may be the kind of guy who can't seem to embrace commitment to one person. Maybe you start to get emotionally or physically close to someone and end up running for the hills. Perhaps the idea of anyone in your space or sharing your life makes you feel trapped. These are signs of *counterdependency*.

Now that you've worked on clarifying what you do want in different relationships, you're ready to look at some common less-than-healthy relationship patterns. Take a moment to clear out the behavioral cobwebs that keep you from the intimacy you deserve and truly desire.

Forget the stereotypes you've heard: "Men are counterdependent; they avoid commitment and closeness and are less emotional. Women are codependent; they're overemotional, clingy, and lose themselves in the relationship." Some of these stereotypes have arisen due to our social upbringing, maybe even from some genetic disposition. Gay and bisexual men are sometimes thought to tend toward counterdependency (as are all men) in their relationships. However, contrary to the stereotype, any man can be codependent, as well.

What is true for you in love relationships? When it comes to sharing your emotions and speaking your truth, do you tend to avoid closeness or act distant (counterdependent)? Or are you more clingy and emotionally needy, tending to let others determine what you want (codependent)? Are you somewhere in between?

For example, Harris wrote: "Closeness is my ultimate goal, but I become codependent in love relationships. I've been a people pleaser and peacemaker most of my life with friends and family, so I don't think I trust myself in terms of meeting my own needs. I tend to hook up with guys I see as "masculine," in control, and able to turn me on. I definitely give up my wants and personal power too easily."

What about your behavior when it comes to other aspects of a relationship, like financial responsibility, daily chores, social interaction, social activities, or fidelity? Do you tend to take on too much responsibility (codependent) or are you a "rejecter," tending to be fiercely independent and separate (counterdependent)? Do these words even fit for you at all? Can you use other, more positive, less "psychobabblish" words?

What is your style in friendships? How do you act in terms of codependency or counterdependency (or whatever words you've chosen to use)?

_____

_____

_____

_____

During your childhood, who contributed to your particular style (parents, siblings, peers, and so on)? How?

_____

_____

_____

_____

What life experiences or other factors have influenced your behavior in relationships (your own personality, your beliefs about the world or others, your homo- or bisexuality)?

_____

_____

_____

_____

Defining Your Likes, Dislikes, and What You Want to Change

Now it's time to take what you have discovered about your style of relating to others and clarify what you feel good about and not so good about. Then you will use this knowledge to avoid co- and counterdependent relationships. Your goal is to move in the direction of healthy *interdependence*, which means that you can be independent, yet dependent on another in times of need. Healthy interdependence allows you to

- Be flexible in your roles

- Be assertive when you feel strongly about something

- Agree to disagree

- Remain clear about "where you stop and the other person begins"

- Take responsibility for your feelings and actions

- Lean on other people for a while

- Trade off who's in charge

In the following chart, list the characteristics you've noticed about yourself and how you behave in relationships, and enter an *F* or an *L* in the second column to indicate if you display these qualities in friendships or love relationships (or both). You might want to think about specific past relationships to guide your learning process. Some examples of characteristics are romantic; self-centered; giving; too needy; closed off; passive about my needs and wants—you get the idea. Then check the appropriate column to show whether you like or dislike these feelings or behaviors in yourself. Next, go through the list and circle the ones you want to change (the "dislikes" you checked). In the last column, write in what you would like to do instead. For example, "too needy" might become "Don't take nonverbal messages too personally. Stop trying to read people's minds."

Take a few minutes to imagine a scene in a past or current relationship (preferably a love relationship) or focus on an imaginary relationship. See yourself acting the way you want. Using the characteristics and behaviors you identified in the chart, visualize yourself behaving in the new way. Let your fantasy of yourself include the qualities you already like in addition to your new desired characteristics.

Remember to practice—in your mind and your real behavior. Like a successful athlete who trains his brain as well as his body, rehearse in your mind the actions and behaviors you want, over and over, to shape your behavior and make it more automatic.

Work on fine-tuning your healthy interdependent behaviors. And don't bother wasting your energy worrying about what you haven't changed yet. Give it time or give it a rest for a while, support yourself to stay on track and let your innate healthy behaviors kick in. Talk to friends and get feedback to fine-tune your best qualities and continue to be patient with your new ones that may still be awkward.

Characteristic	Friendship or Love?	I Like It	I Don't Like It	How I Can Change It

There's No Better Time Than Now

Your future is determined by what you do today. So if you haven't already, start building relationships that support your love for people and life, your values and passions, and the kind of intimacy your heart yearns for. As you move through your everyday coming-out process, it's likely you will lose some friends, renew your relationships with others, and if all goes well, meet new, loving and supportive friends and lovers.

As a GBQ man, building healthy relationships can be more challenging due to limited opportunities for seeing healthy relationships and the stigmatization and isolation of GBQ people. Here are a few suggestions to help you get more of what you want in your daily life and avoid negative relationship snafus:

- Remember: You are in charge of how you want to be.

- Check up on and alter your self-limiting thoughts and feelings.

- Take courage from the fact that gay and bisexual men are, by their nature and from adversity, survivors.

- Your past style simply influences your patterns of behavior; it doesn't doom you to a life of being codependent, counterdependent, or whatever.

- If you tend to get stuck when trying to make the changes you want in your behavior, talk to a friend about it, read some self-help books about your particular issues, or see a therapist trained to work with gay and bisexual relationships.

- Look for models of what you want in relationships and personal interaction.

- Avoid people who are currently abusing substances.

Being out is not always an easy task, but I'm happy to report to you that by and large it's worth it. If you continue to be honest and genuine with yourself and others, you will be blessed with all the emotional richness that life can offer you. As a GBQ man, your relationships will be more meaningful and more rewarding, and you will find the means to build a community of friends and loved ones to sustain you through all the trials and tribulations in your life.

12

Here's to Your Sexual Health

*We have learned and will continue to learn how to increase
self-respect and enrich relationships by sanely meeting our
sexual needs.*

—Don Clark, *Loving Someone Gay*

A book that explores issues relating to sexual orientation would be incomplete without a discussion about sex. So it's time to turn your attention towards your sexual health—physical and emotional. In previous chapters you read about ways to tune into and improve your psychological well-being by recognizing your healthy and unhealthy thought patterns. You've also examined your specific needs and identified barriers against having and developing relationships. In this chapter you'll explore issues that are present throughout this book as they relate specifically to sex, such as self-respect, self-esteem, unhealthy patterns, and honest communication.

Your Physical Sexual Health

Guarding your physical sexual health means, simply, using protective sexual practices to avoid direct contact with bodily fluids that carry significant concentrations of the HIV virus or other sexually transmitted diseases. You know that it can be fatal to deny that you're at risk. So if you're thinking, "I'll never get AIDS," or making decisions based on thoughts like "This guy seems safe to me," you are likely putting yourself in sexually risky situations. Allow scientific evidence, not foolish bravado, to guide your thinking and behavior. The intent of this section is not to make you overly self-conscious but to help you become more aware of your sexual decisions and actions in order to stay physically and psychologically healthy. Make healthy choices. "Don't play with your life," I tell my clients. "You only get one."

Protecting Your Sexual Health in the Age of AIDS

Nearly everyone has experienced, in one way or another, the suffering caused by HIV and AIDS. HIV is without a doubt the most frightening of modern-day sexual threats to physical health.

While sexually transmitted diseases (STDs) such as gonorrhea and syphilis are prevalent, they are easily diagnosed and treated by modern medicine. And although genital herpes has no cure (just medicines to help with outbreaks), causes painful lesions and discomfort, and is easily transmitted to others, it is not a fatal disease. Hepatitis (A and B) had many men scared in the 1980s but both strains may be preventable for the most part with vaccinations.

Although HIV-infected people are living longer and healthier lives with the help of antiviral and prophylactic medications, AIDS and the accompanying opportunistic infections are most often the deadly consequence of the HIV virus.

Here's what we know about HIV: Tears, saliva, and urine have low concentrations of the virus; blood, cervical secretions, sperm, and seminal fluid have high concentrations. What constitutes risk depends on whether HIV is present, the amount present in the particular fluid (for example, blood has the highest concentration of HIV), and the receptor sites, among other factors. The following is a rough summary of the spectrum of risky activities based on information from the AIDS Center for Disease Control Hotline and the San Francisco AIDS Foundation:

Unsafe/Risky

- Insertive or receptive intercourse without a condom

- Vaginal or rectal intercourse without a condom

- Blood contact

- Oral sex without a condom (semen or urine in the mouth)

- Sharing sex toys that have contact with bodily fluids

- Anal rimming

Variable Risk

- Vaginal or rectal intercourse with a condom

- Oral sex with a condom*
- Oral sex without a condom, before any fluid exchange*

Probably Safe

- Tongue/deep kissing (risky if cuts or sores are present in mouth)

Safe (no exchange of bodily fluids)

- Massaging, hugging, and cuddling
- Mutual masturbation (may be unsafe if cuts or sores are present)
- Rubbing
- Voyeurism, exhibitionism
- Fantasizing
- Dry kissing

* Oral sex and HIV-infection risk is controversial and continues to be debated and studied as to if it is "more" or "less" risky.

Note: Information on HIV risk continues to be updated. Be smart; research for yourself what you need to do to be sexually safe.

Remember that monogamous sex does not guarantee you will not encounter the HIV virus. So get tested, talk about it, know your partner and his or her status, and then use safer sex practices *anyway*. There's always the possibility of finding out too late that someone whom you've been assured is uninfected will turn out to be positive. And there's always the possibility that a partner assumed to be monogamous will be secretly unfaithful and thus put you at risk. Unfortunately, agreements between human beings, whether implicit or explicit, are sometimes broken.

> **FYI:**
> Although there's no scientific proof yet, there seems to be a relationship between having positive feelings about one's sexual orientation, along with a sense of community with other bi and gay men, and having attitudes and beliefs that foster HIV risk reduction (Herek and Glunt 1995).

Manage Your Sexual Behavior

To help you manage sexual disease risks you should familiarize yourself with some of the myths and truths about dangerous sexual behavior. Unfortunately, increasing your knowledge of HIV/AIDS, fearing illness or death, or recognizing that sexual behavior and emotional responses are not easily changed are, by themselves, insufficient to avoid unsafe practices (Landau-Stanton et al. 1993). All this knowledge can help, but you must be willing to practice the art of self-preservation each and every time you enter a potential sex scene.

> Think . . . *think* . . . **think** before acting. Have safer sex in *all* circumstances— no excuses.

You can help yourself most in the STD arena by recognizing and admitting your human vulnerability. Try to be aware of the excuses you make and the myths you believe in that perpetuate any risky sexual behavior, as well as the frustrations you may feel about the limits put on your sexual behavior with others. Armed with this knowledge, you can recognize your own rationalizations and accept the reality of HIV risk before it gets you. Especially important is to admit the power your sexual passions can exert over rational decision making. Here are some additional ways to increase your awareness, reduce your risk of disease, and improve your ability to make healthy decisions:

- Talk about HIV/AIDS with others, especially potential partners.

- Work with HIV-positive people.

- Avoid drugs and alcohol when in sexually provocative situations.

- Always be prepared with a lot of condoms.

- Recognize the negative influence that shame and homophobia can have on your moods, possibly causing you to engage in risky behavior.

Now add your own ideas about how you can reduce your disease risks and make healthy sexual decisions.

_____

_____

_____

_____

Even if you are already HIV positive, there is scientific evidence to suggest you should still practice safe sex to prevent reinfecting yourself with disease, increasing the viral load, and/or exposing yourself to other strains or possible resistant forms of disease.

Train Yourself for Safer Sex Practices

Imagine taking a personal video moment of yourself and a partner right before a hot, passionate sexual encounter. In addition to the passion, such moments are also difficult decision-making situations. You can enhance your image by placing new, safer sex practices in the same video moment. Say out loud some clear self-talk right now. Make these activities something you can and will actually be able to do in the heat of the moment. For example, see yourself with a condom, enjoying the eroticism of putting the condom on. Hear yourself saying "No" to acts that are not safe, imagining the specter of HIV/AIDS looming over the immediate, unsafe act of passion.

Now spend some time thinking of what will really help *you* to create positive sexually safer practices—both before and during emotional and sexually exciting moments. Write your ideas down and commit to using them.

_____

_____

_____

_____

Sex and Your Emotions

There's no denying it: Psychological health is incomplete without including sex in the mix. So you need to learn to identify what turns you on and what is sexually healthy for you.

What does emotional sexual health mean to you as a GBQ man?

_____

_____

_____

_____

As a GBQ man, how do aspects of emotional health overlap with issues of your physical health when it comes to having sex?

_____

_____

_____

_____

Consider fine-tuning your emotional sexual health if you

- Relate to people sexually as objects
- Are sexual without any respect for other's needs
- Use power differences (like age, employment, wealth, size, intelligence) to take advantage of others sexually
- Are not mutually consenting in sexual relationships
- Are disrespectful, hurtful, or abusive in your sexual practices

- Spend excessive amounts of time preoccupied with finding and having sex

If you're not doing any of these don'ts, you're likely to be somewhere in the ballpark of what is considered sexually healthy. But if you do fit somewhere in these less-than-sexually-healthy categories, don't wait any longer before finding yourself some outside help. Attend a Sex and Love Addicts Anonymous group; see a psychotherapist who specializes in sexual disorders or issues; or join a therapy group with others who have similar issues. You may also be able to find some books specific to your sexual conflicts, but my experience shows that some solid outside help (that is, a person who is experienced in dealing with these issues) is needed to break those unhealthy patterns. Objectivity is necessary to facilitate most change, and objectivity is pretty hard to have with your own sexual issues.

Promoting Sexual Self-Esteem

You've already done some important work in earlier chapters on the issues of shame and internalized homophobia and how those hang-ups can keep you from being comfortable with your sexuality. Keep in mind that balancing sex and intimacy keeps you in touch with your heart as well as your groin. Obsessive and compulsive sexual activity interferes with a healthy sexual emotional state. It is sure to sabotage close intimate relationships, and in general can damage healthy balance in other areas of your life.

Many sexual disorders, such as premature ejaculation and impotence, are commonly associated with psychological factors such as performance anxiety. For GBQ men, feelings of inadequacy, internalized homophobia, self-recrimination, and religious guilt can all be just as powerful as performance anxiety in interference with sexual functioning. On the other hand, there are many ways to contribute to good sexual functioning. You can nurture your confidence in your own sexual identity. You can seek out and develop relationships with GBQ peers and your GBQ community. You can be out in positive ways, act in physically healthy ways, and develop a reservoir of positive sexual self-talk.

Try to identify some positive thoughts and behaviors that will promote your sexual self-esteem and health. Here are a few ideas to get you thinking:

- Feel sure of myself and my sexual desires
- Use POM thinking (see chapter 6) to challenge my homophobic thoughts and accept that they are only thoughts and do not create my reality
- Support my own erotic feelings without analyzing them too much

- Respect and honor the other person's desires as well as my own

- Know that I can be sexual and still avoid STDs and HIV

- Engage in safer sex practices, to honor and respect my body and life

- Have my own view of what it means to be a man despite the opinions of others

- Get out of the closet, to clarify my thinking and keep myself sexually whole and honest

Balancing Sex and Intimacy, Joy and Pleasure

[A]s long as I kept them apart, love would be sexless and sex loveless. . . .

—Paul Monette, *Becoming a Man*

One of the greatest joys of coming out can be exploring your sexual feelings and erotic desires—by yourself and with others. Whether you're twenty, forty-five, or eighty-five, knowing you are free to be yourself opens up a multitude of possibilities. You get the opportunity to shed all those old admonitions and experience the thrill of touching another person's body or fantasizing about a guy or gal who turns you on. Just as you go through various stages of emotional development and physical growth, so can your sexual desires grow and change.

Changes in your sexual excitement levels and the extent to which you more fully experience your erotic, sensual side are influenced by some of the following factors:

- Where you are in the coming-out stages

- Where you are in your life cycle

- Your capacity for psychological and spiritual growth, both of which deepen your understanding of who you are and what you need

- The transitions of your friendships and your sexual and love relationships

- Your body image, which affects your confidence about you and your physique

- Physical changes that affect your health and self-image

Sexual feelings and desires are not stagnant. Sexual interests are part of your evolving self. This is not to suggest there is something wrong with you if you like the same things you liked five years ago. But you may want to check in with yourself as a GBQ man to see if you have fallen into a fantasy rut or settled into some patterns that prevent you from expressing new creative ways to be pleasured and give pleasure.

Take Stock of Your Sexual Desires

Many GBQ men are first aware of having same-sex yearnings as early as five years old. If you look back on yourself as a kid who began to have feelings for the same or both sexes, you can probably remember what gave you that special sexual charge—even if you didn't have a name for it back then or you were confused by the sensations in your body. You might think of this as the beginning of your attempts to come to terms with your real gay or bisexual self.

When and how did you first know you had feelings for the same and/or opposite sex? Write about your first memory of gay or bisexual inclinations.

_____

_____

_____

_____

Even if it took you many years, perhaps into adulthood, to recognize your gay or bisexual desires, you probably knew deep inside what really turned you on. Coming to terms with your sexual interests as a GBQ man means being open to growth. It also means you accept the consistent underlying themes that inform your identity as a gay or bisexual man. You'll need to continue exploring what turns you on, accepting that feelings will probably evolve and that you may eventually integrate sex, love, and intimacy. In addition, you may still have to face and fend off internal and external homophobia.

As a GBQ adult you may have felt confused about your sexual yearnings and desires, especially if you have been told that being gay or bisexual is "bad," or if you were sexually abused. If so, you may find that your mixed emotions may still get in the way of pursuing or experiencing gay or bisexual pleasures.

What holds you back, if anything, from pursuing physical relationships with men or women?

_____

_____

_____

_____

Coming to terms with your sexual desires is a part of learning to accept yourself as ever-evolving. And as you change, so might your desires. Ed, for example, was feeling bored with his sex life. He was dating guys who were sexy, but distant. He started asking guys out who were interesting to him on an emotional level; he also began to experiment with his romantic side (candles, hot baths, and massages). He found he was just as turned on, but on a new level.

Take a moment to ask yourself if you are pleased with your current sexual desires. How would you change them?

_____

_____

_____

_____

What else could you change about your sexual desires that will lead to more fulfillment?

_____

_____

_____

_____

Are there specific ways in which you deny your sexual desires? Henry, for example, found that he was still secretive about his sexual turn-ons. He began to make a habit of masturbating and using pornography instead of allowing himself to try to meet someone. What, if anything, do you still need to do to come to terms with and enjoy your sexual desires?

_____

_____

_____

_____

Talk about Sex

If you haven't already discovered it, talking about sex is fun! It is liberating and amusing to talk with trusted friends about sex, telling stories about past encounters (or ongoing ones), laughing at silly sexual innuendos, and asking each other "truth or dare" kinds of questions. What was the craziest place you ever made love? The riskiest situation you ever had? Who was your first? What were some of your early fantasies? Of course, it's up to you how much "truth" you give away, but these conversations help affirm that your erotic desires are okay. You have some fun, and you get to challenge your own myths.

For many a GBQ man, it's kind of like being an adolescent again, except without as much fear of being rejected or ostracized. Take Isaac, for example. He gets together with Sue and Brandon every Thursday; someone inevitably starts sharing about his or her latest date or sex interest. They end up hooting and hollering about some of their more intimate times, oohing and aahing over exotic locations of past interludes, and making lewd references to their body parts. They have made sure, though, to create a safe space for this fun, by agreeing not to tease one another or share the information with others.

Such sharing is not for everyone. And mutual trust is crucial. You also have to know and respect one another's boundaries. Having friendly sexual confidantes can be a great way to loosen up your psyche, reduce secrecy and shame, and have some fun with sex. Check it out; try to find or create some safe situations for these discussions, with people you trust. If you don't have such people in your life, try keeping a journal of your sexual fantasies or encounters (and put it in a safe place!).

Do you have anyone with whom you might be able to have some fun and share your sexual escapades or fantasies? If so, who?

_____

_____

_____

_____

How can you create a safe space—either for yourself alone, or with others—to share some of your more intimate sexual details?

_____

_____

_____

_____

Talking to a Lover

Couples often struggle with how to discuss sexual issues with one another. It's certainly a touchy subject and can make for an awkward situation. But it's healthy to talk about sex, though at times it means stretching your comfort zones. You will find that speaking up about sex not only increases your chance for intimacy but can ease tension in your love relationships.

Imagine talking to a lover about your sexual relationship. The lover could be someone you are seeing now or someone you have dated in the past or would like to date in the future.

What would you say?

_____

_____

_____

How would you like to act?

_____

_____

_____

How would you like the other person to respond?

_____

_____

_____

How wouldn't you like the other person to respond?

_____

_____

_____

It's important to identify not only what you like but what you dislike as well. That way if someone says or does something that makes you uncomfortable you can be better prepared to deal with it. Remember to respect yourself in all aspects of sex—if your lover says something you don't like, speak up and make your opinion known.

Sex and Intimacy—the Delicate Balance

Intimacy is about emotional, intellectual, and sexual closeness. It can help you create a genuine sense of belonging and authenticity and can heal past wounds, yet intimacy requires patience; it doesn't happen overnight and it doesn't happen without some effort.

What does intimacy mean to you?

_____

_____

_____

_____

Enjoying pure, unadulterated sex can be essential to reducing your inhibitions about being gay or bisexual. It can also be quite a rush. But there's an old saying about "too much of a good thing" that holds a lot of truth. Too much sex can result in boredom; addictive patterns, such as dependency or compulsions; or too much time and energy spent looking for the next "fix" to get you off. You will benefit by being aware of when you are using sex compulsively. Watch out for patterns of escape or avoidance; instead strive for healthy expressions of pleasure, affection, and love.

Mark used to go to a beach where a lot of gay cruising went on. He knew that he could have instant sex if he wanted it, and frequently went to the beach when he was horny or just wanted to relieve some stress. This became a problem for Mark, though, as he began to avoid more meaningful connections with people. He found he was spending more time at the beach and neglecting a lot of his work and home responsibilities. He began to realize that the sex in these encounters, though immediate and exciting, was also shallow and gratuitous, leaving him feeling even emptier than before.

I'm not here to step up on a soapbox and tell you how much is too much, or what you should or should not do. Nor is this discussion about morality, shame, or guilt. I encourage you to use this section as an opportunity to develop the right balance for yourself. Avoid judging yourself and your behavior. If you find that you're experiencing anger or other discomforting feelings as you answer the questions, stop and look inside. Are there some negative voices that you're listening to? Is your internal critic passing judgment? Are you listening to the voice of internalized homophobia created by past experiences? Are you feeling defensive about some sexual imbalance that you suspect isn't good for you as a GBQ man?

What, if anything, would you like to change about your reactions to sex, pleasure, and intimacy?

_____

_____

_____

_____

Like most things in life, sex in moderation can provide a sense of health and well-being—both physical and emotional. Mark's behavior is one illustration of how a person can lose balance in his sexual life. At the other extreme, a total lack of sexual activity (although typical for some people) can be the result of feeling shame or guilt about having same-sex desires, being out of touch with or ashamed of your body, or lacking experience with or respect for sensual desires. A healthy respect for sexual pleasure and joy, in addition to respecting your own desires, can facilitate a deeper connection to your soul and self. It will also help you achieve a balance between give and take with others. Besides knowing what you want sexually, knowing what turns you off can help you deepen your ability to respect yourself in sexual encounters. What turns you off about a person sexually? What sexual acts turn you off? How would you like to address them with a sex partner? What would you say or do? How would you time this?

In some cases, a loss of sexual desire or functioning may indicate that you are experiencing side effects from medicine, a hormonal imbalance (although this is rare), or some other physical problems. If this is your case, take some time to check it out with your primary care physician or a specialist in urogenital medicine.

How Much Sex Is Enough?

Use the following scale to rate where you think you are in terms of balance between too much and not enough sexual activity. Make your estimation in comparison to what you think you want at this point in your life. Try to be honest. This is a subjective, personal rating, not a comparison with someone else.

0	2	4	6	8	10
Not Enough		Enough			Too Much

I am a _____ on the scale.

How do you feel about where you are on the scale? Do you want to change your balance?

_____

_____

_____

What would be "enough" for you?

_____

_____

_____

If you put yourself closest to Not Enough on the scale, go through the following list and check what might help you move closer to Enough.

_____ Masturbate more often (I really won't go blind or be struck down by God)

_____ Initiate sex more frequently

_____ Go to places where I can meet people who are my type

_____ Expand my sexual repertoire; try new sexual activities

_____ See a physician about a physical problem I have

_____ Open my mind and be more flexible about seeing sex as positive

_____ Improve my body image

_____ Work on my shame issues and self-judgement

_____ Rent some videos to get some ideas of the kind of sex I like

_____ Work on my abuse issues

_____ Get massages on a regular basis to get back in touch with my body

_____ Exercise more regularly

_____ Work on my fear of HIV and learn more about safe sex practices

_____ _____

_____ _____

_____ _____

If you put yourself closest to Too Much, go through the following list and check what might help you to move closer to Enough.

_____ Masturbate less often (I really can overdo it)

_____ Limit the number of people I have sex with

_____ Limit how often I pursue sex

_____ Get to know people better before making any moves

_____ Learn to delay gratification

_____ Be more particular about who is my type

_____ Become closer to my partner

_____ Develop hobbies that I really enjoy

_____ Try some healthier sensation-seeking activities, such as scuba diving or biking

_____ Join a support group, such as Sex and Love Addicts Anonymous

_____ Consult a physician about a physical problem I have

_____ Open my mind to other enjoyable activities

_____ Work to feel better about myself in areas other than sex and sexuality

_____ Work on my shame issues and self-judgments

_____ See a therapist about my compulsions

_____ Read some books on my issues about sex

_____ Work on my abuse issues

_____ Get massages on a regular basis to get back in touch with my body

_____ Exercise more regularly

_____ _____

_____ _____

_____ _____

Now take a look at the things you've checked. What specifically can you do to better meet your needs for balancing sex and intimacy? For example, if you checked "Improve my body image," you may write down, "Stop comparing myself to models in magazines. Start a daily exercise routine. Eat more vegetables and less ice cream!" Or, if you checked "Learn to delay gratification," you could write, "Wait twenty minutes before reacting to my impulses—see if they pass."

_____

_____

_____

_____

What specific coping strategies would help you enjoy gay or bisexual sex more? (Examples: learn to relax; accept my body; come out to others.)

_____

_____

_____

_____

Being Well and Being Single

"I want to be in a relationship but I don't meet people very easily."

"It's tough out there. I don't think I'll ever meet the right guy for me."

"This town is unfriendly."

"There are *no* guys my type—where are they?"

"I don't like the bar scene."

"There is nothing to do for GBQ men here."

"I'm afraid of having sex and getting HIV, so I don't even risk being sexual."

"The grass always seems to be greener on the other side."

"Commitment scares me, so why not just have anonymous sex?"

Statements like these are typical of men expressing concerns about being single and GBQ. It's a situation that includes loneliness, stress, and anxiety for just about anyone. Being a single man may bring forth worries about being on your own, problems with meeting others, feelings of isolation from people in general, and—of course—concerns about safe sex. If you're a single GBQ man, you may benefit from putting the joys and stresses of being single and dating into perspective, as well as improving your interpersonal skills.

Being single is certainly not the worst thing in the world, but it can be a painful experience if you desperately want to be in a relationship. It doesn't help, either, if you're shy, hate the single scene, or have few ways to meet other GBQ men. Or maybe you've dated a lot and are frustrated by so many mismatches.

It's a good idea to remember that being in a relationship is perhaps too often stressed as the ultimate goal for all single people. You may enjoy being on your own for the time being. If you don't want a relationship right now, don't feel there is something wrong with you. Don't get forced onto the path of somebody else's expectation that you have to pair up in order to be truly whole. Being independent and self-sufficient can be a healthy way of living your life.

With that said, let's move on to a discussion about getting some practice meeting the people you want to meet.

Open Up to New People

If you tend to be the kind of person who is shy or whose voice quivers and heart quakes with the thought of meeting someone for the first time, you may need some help accepting your anxiety, learning how to relax more, and developing tools to comfortably meet and socialize with others. If you are too set in your ways, have narrowed your point of view by requiring specific qualities in others, or trip yourself up by talking too much about yourself or being controlling of others, you may need a social tune-up to be a more effective communicator. Any of these factors can distance you from others. Such obstacles to healthy social interaction may be holding you back, but you may not even be aware they exist. They manifest themselves in behaviors and attitudes that send the message that you are not interested or emotionally unavailable for a relationship.

For example, Chris was a caring, compassionate man in his early twenties who was shy and lacked self-confidence in social situations. He had a way of holding his body in a protective, closed-off manner. In conversations, he often spoke with a haughty, "intellectual" tone that lacked warmth (even though that's not what he wanted to communicate) and made him seem invulnerable. The vibes people got from him were that he was not interested in being close or personal with others. With the help of a good friend, Chris began to recognize what he was doing and started to actively monitor the messages he was unconsciously communicating. He made an effort to act in ways that were more engaging, trying to show interest in others and invite personal conversation. Chris even enlisted a buddy of his to help him stay on track and wink at him when he slipped into old habits.

What would you like to change about your personality or style of relating to others? How can you make yourself more emotionally available to meet interesting men or women?

If you think this section applies especially to you, now might be a good time to go back and review chapters 5 and 11. They contain suggestions for meeting interesting new people, such as through other friends, on the internet, via ads in your local gay/bi community rag, and so forth.

First and foremost, and as emphasized throughout this book, try to get comfortable with being single. If you can accept that it's okay to be a single GBQ man, you're more likely to be less needy. In turn, you'll be less demanding of perfection and more objective about deciding who is a healthy match for you.

The next step, if you're serious about meeting someone who is right for you, is to examine your relationship and communication skills closely and honestly. Somewhere in this process, you'll also have to explore new networks and avenues for meeting others. And practice, practice, practice being your best. Sure, some people are really good at it: They meet others easily and naturally, seeming to have a special charisma that attracts people like a magnet. Some people have a knack for intimate relationships. Some men have developed a comfortable interpersonal style that is easy to be around. But if you're in the majority, you probably don't fit into these lucky categories. Don't despair—with persistence, you *can* meet and communicate with relationship-worthy people.

Here are a few suggestions for the single GBQ man seeking healthy relationships. (It's likely that you've heard some of these before!)

- Check your ideals—are they broad enough? Are you eliminating possible dates because of unimportant "surface" characteristics such as physique, financial standing, or social status?

- Don't make snap judgments or turn up your nose up at other people's differences. This attitude is unattractive and creates distance and mistrust.

- Trust your intuition, but also be thoughtful. Take the time to find out whether you might click with someone.

- When you really don't like someone or feel excessively uncomfortable with a new date, move on. Wish the person a happy, prosperous life and move on.

- Be open to getting to know people *before* you decide you want to date them.

- Learn to listen. Be curious about the people you meet.

- Identify what you might be doing to push people away.

- Identify some ways you are already effective in bringing people close to you.

- Know your anxieties; they may be creating feelings of uneasiness in others.

- Fine-tune your body language. Practice assertive body communication, friendly eye contact, and warm facial expressions.

- Use your own areas of interests to link with other people's areas of interest.

- Ask for feedback from friends about how you come across and be prepared to look honestly at your style of interrelating.

- Work on being the kind of man with whom *you* would want to be in love.

13

Beyond Discrimination

How annoyed I am with Society for wasting my time by making homosexuality criminal. The subterfuges, the self-consciousness that might have been avoided.

—E. M. Forster, *The Gay Almanac*

This chapter takes a closer look at some of the forces that can either blow you off course or help you remain solid in your commitment to your personal GBQ journey. Although you probably don't think of your sexual orientation as a "choice" you've made, you'll find you do have to make choices about reactions to your sexual orientation. Homophobia and discrimination are facts of life, and you'll always have to think about whom to associate with, whom to be open with, when to respond to rudeness and hatefulness, and when to bite your tongue when you most want to stick it out. The forces of homophobia, community assimilation, prejudice, and discrimination may shake and intimidate even the most comfortably out GBQ man.

In this chapter you'll get some help with clarifying your feelings, thoughts, and values about these challenges. If you make some decisions ahead of time about how to meet adversity, you're ahead of the game. An ounce of prevention is worth a pound of cure, right?

Getting Beyond Homophobia

In Greek mythology, Hercules slew Hydra, the many-headed serpent. Unfortunately, you have your own modern-day Hydra. As the hero of your journey, you will face the multifarious evil of homophobia many times before it's conquered. You've already read about internalized homophobia in chapter 7. You studied ways of managing internal fears about your sexual orientation. When you can win your internal battles, you'll be in a good position to deal objectively and authoritatively with the external battles.

Consider the following quote—an unfortunate but classic example of homophobia: "The poor homosexuals—they have declared war upon nature, and now nature is exacting an awful retribution." This statement was uttered by Patrick Buchanan, American conservative and 1996 presidential candidate.

How do you feel when you read what Buchanan said? What do you think about such attitudes?

_____

_____

_____

_____

Do you have trouble believing that these attitudes (or people) exist? If so, that probably means you're one of the lucky GBQ men whose exposure to intolerance and prejudice has been minimal, or at least manageable. But believe it: These people—long on judgment and short on truth—are out there. As long as there are oppressive religions and cultures; as long as there are unenlightened teachers and preachers who command that homosexuality is wrong; as long as there are racists and bigots, fear and ignorance, jealousy and hate, and insecurity, there will be homophobia.

Homophobia is something you'll need to face. I urge you to gather your supports around you; try to find constructive ways to educate those who are misinformed and challenge those who aim to hurt or punish. Of course if you're constantly worrying about all the differences of opinion and meanness in the world, you'll never get your work done, your animals won't get fed, your fun time will be spoiled, and your laundry and dishes will pile up into a big, moldy mess. But because homophobia exists and must be acknowledged, your goal will be to *get beyond it* and not let it have power in your life.

Sometimes getting beyond homophobia means you have to write a few people off. Sometimes you must take a stand to let them know they're misinformed. Sometimes you'll be able to muster up the love and compassion to take time to educate them, but there will likely be few about whom you care enough to do that. Sometimes getting beyond homophobia means taking on more responsibility to fight it, perhaps by being more active in community or political gay and bisexual issues.

A Personal Story

After years of living as an out gay man, I am still amazed and troubled when homophobia rears its ugly head from unlikely places and in unlikely forms. I am lucky to live in California, in a relatively open-minded (if not necessarily politically liberal) community that is accepting of diversity. Even here, however, reality sometimes brings me roughly back to earth. Not too long ago, at a board of supervisors meeting in Santa Clara County, the issue of domestic partner registration was under consideration. I was astonished to encounter an elementary school–age child in the crowd of antireferendum protesters carrying a sign that read, "Please don't molest me." I cannot help but marvel at the things people choose to teach their children.

How to Respond to Homophobia

Go back now and reread what you wrote about your feelings and attitudes toward Buchanan's statement and what it represents. These feelings and thoughts are your clues to understanding your role in dealing with homophobia. Your internal reactions and logic can guide you to understand what (and whom) you are meeting when homophobia shows up at your front door or knocks you down in the street when you're walking along minding your own business.

Did you write about feeling angry at Buchanan's words? That's healthy. Are you frightened by this attitude? That's normal, as well. In fact, all your feelings are valid here; you just get to make some choices about what to do with them.

Look at Your Past Responses

Try to think of a recent homophobic remark that was made to you. It doesn't matter if this incident seems minor, write about it anyway. Who was the offender? Where were you?

_____

_____

_____

_____

If you can't think of anything, use this hypothetical example and think through your probable responses: A co-worker who doesn't know you're GBQ says to you, "Homos and bisexuals are all a bunch of sex-craving, morally corrupt, weak people."

_____

_____

_____

_____

Validate your feelings by putting pen to paper. How do you feel and what do you think about what happened?

_____

_____

_____

_____

What did you say or do in response? Were you happy with the way you responded? Why or why not?

_____

_____

_____

_____

What, if anything, would you do differently if this incident happened tomorrow, either in the way you handled your feelings or the way you responded?

_____

_____

_____

_____

Choose Your Responses

How can you handle incidents of bigotry and prejudice about your sexuality? Here are a few ideas to help you with homophobic encounters.

- Remember that you always have a choice of whether or not to respond. Don't feel you have to respond to anyone's prejudice, hatred, or abuse.

- Decide whether you're safe from physical harm. You probably should choose not to respond to someone in the following circumstances: The person is a stranger; you're in unknown territory, such as a less-than-friendly part of town or an unfamiliar city or setting; you're alone; you feel unsafe in some way; you don't have an escape plan. In general, these situations are probably not worth your time and energy—you may just be "lowering yourself to their level." You may even be risking your life.

- Ask yourself, "Do I care enough about what was said or about this person to respond?"

- If the person is close to you and you care and want to maintain a connection with them, tell them how their statement makes you feel. Be specific; clarify what you think. You might say that you think their opinion is based on a lack of knowledge of what it is to be GBQ, or that bigotry and discrimination are unacceptable values to you, or that they are harmful acts based on a lack of knowledge, etc.

- Ask the person how he or she has become informed with such knowledge. Ask if he or she is aware of the effects of such views on others.

- If you really want to discuss what was said, ask the person to repeat their statement or opinion. Break it down into specific points and discuss them one at a time. For example, in the situation provided earlier, you'd want to address each supposed characteristic of gay people—sex-craving; morally corrupt; and weak.

- Trust your intuition about how to respond, but it's always best to remain calm and not let your insecurities or emotions get the best of you. Above all, stay in charge of what you say and do and keep it simple.

- Afterward, talk it out. Discuss what happened with people who share your feelings, thoughts, and experiences. Don't let it settle in your mind as something to be ashamed of; don't cultivate it as a hurtful wound.

- If the person is able to see your point of view, great. If not, move on, despite any hurt you may feel. Don't let disappointment in the outcome of any confrontation of homophobia take your confidence away. Avoid becoming a victim to someone else's ignorance.

Twenty-year-old Marco had just begun to come out as a gay man. He was out with a friend at a local bar and grill. Three guys at the next table noticed their physical closeness and began to make rude and hurtful remarks loud enough for Marco and his friend to hear.

What would you do if you were Marco?

_____

_____

_____

_____

    Marco and his friend decided to complain to the manager. After they left the restaurant, Marco talked about his feelings with his friend but was still upset about it. He decided to write his thoughts in his journal. He wrote a list of positive reasons to be out and proud as a gay man. He also wrote out a plan for future encounters: "I will practice resisting the influence of others who want to change the way I look, act, and feel. When homophobia rears its ugly head, I will write and talk about its effects on me and my friends. I won't let those idiots bring me down—it's their issue not mine."

Now that you've read the suggestions for choosing your response to homophobia, return to what you wrote about your past responses. What, if anything, would you do differently?

_____

_____

_____

_____

In general, what are some ways you want to "get beyond" homophobia? How can you release any hold homophobia may have on your life? (Examples: Speak up whenever I feel it is safe to do so; Stop trying to change all the jerks of the world; Don't give homophobia any energy it doesn't deserve.)

_____

_____

_____

_____

Make a decision here and now: What will you actively do to prepare yourself for handling homophobia, whether it emerges from your internal self or your external world of acquaintances, friends, family, culture, and society?

_____

_____

For some additional reading on the subject of homophobia and prejudice, I recommend Betty Berzon's wonderful book, *Setting Them Straight* (1996). It details the background of and some ways to respond to homophobia and bigotry in society and in close relationships.

Discrimination and Prejudice: The Real Shame

We believe that the rights of all people must be protected and guaranteed. We believe that the gay and lesbian community must be supported in their civil rights as well as their right for their sexual preference.

—Coretta Scott King, *The Gay Almanac*

Discrimination against people because of their sexuality occurs every day. Fundamental human rights taken for granted by most people in the United States are often denied to openly gay, lesbian, and bisexual people. Fortunately, groups such as the National Gay and Lesbian Task Force, Human Rights Campaign, and the Lambda Legal Defense Fund in the United States are laboring to change the legal and political playing field by actively lobbying against discriminatory legislative measures. These groups and others are working to introduce bills and constitutional amendments that will guarantee freedom from discrimination based on sexuality.

For the present, however, gay, lesbian, and bisexual individuals in the United States have no such guarantee of employment, domestic partner insurance benefits, medical visitation rights, or housing rights. We do not have the right to visit as a "family member" a partner who is in the hospital. We cannot serve in the military unless we keep our sexual orientation a secret. We cannot get married, adopt a child without suffering major legal encumbrances and social disapproval, or have legal (in some states) oral or anal sex (which is illegal for some heterosexuals, too). All of the latter rights, however, are in the process of being challenged to one degree or another by the National Gay and Lesbian Task Force and the Human Rights Campaign (amongst others).

An additional disadvantage suffered by GBQ people is the misinformation and scare tactics perpetuated by groups such as the Moral Majority and Coalition for Family Values. These organizations, along with conservative religious and political groups led by people such as Pat

Buchanan, Pat Robertson, Lou Sheldon, and Senator Jesse Helms, work to create a climate of fear among the unenlightened public. By targeting and misinforming church members, conservative families, and naivë individuals, they are able to propagate false and biased information that gays, lesbians, and bisexuals want special rights and threaten "family values." There have been several recent attempts to pass anti-gay initiatives in various states—for example, Colorado's approved 1992 Amendment 2, later struck down by the U.S. Supreme Court.

Outing Prejudice

The events and campaigns involving gay, lesbian, and bisexual issues are a call to all GBQ people to be active in some form or fashion for GBQ rights, or we risk losing even basic freedoms. Depending on your personality and your level of commitment, there are many things you can do to lend your heart to the cause: attend protests and marches, contribute to fund-raisers, write letters and sign petitions against discrimination, donate money or volunteer professional skills, and vote and campaign for GBQ-positive political candidates. You can take a stand every day by speaking out—to anyone, including friends, family members, and your next-door neighbor—about human rights and against discrimination of any sort.

Many have compared the current struggle of GBQ people to other battles for human rights. In many ways, our struggle is like the Civil Rights movement of the last three decades; the fight for equal employment and pay rights for women and ethnic minorities; movements toward ordaining women as ministers; and the right to be free from sexual harassment.

How have you been discriminated against because of your sexuality?

_____

_____

_____

_____

Have you subconsciously ignored discrimination and prejudice by remaining in the closet? Write about your feelings regarding this.

_____

_____

_____

_____

When you have experienced discrimination firsthand, or witnessed or learned of other homosexual or bisexual individuals being denied certain freedoms, what is the message you get about being a GBQ man?

_____

_____

_____

_____

What have been the effects—subtle or obvious—on your self-esteem when you have experienced discrimination based on your sexual orientation?

_____

_____

_____

_____

How Much Do You Know about Prejudice?

If you are a person of color *and* GBQ, you are probably far too familiar already with the destructive forces of shame, prejudice, and discrimination. If you are not a member of a so-called minority ethnic group, you may not have experienced much prejudice firsthand. It will benefit you to be better informed. Talk to African Americans about their struggles to attain equal treatment in the workplace and the world in general. Read about their history, and that of other peoples—Asian, Middle Eastern, Native American, East Indian, Jewish—who know discrimination intimately. Talk to women and ask them what discrimination feels like; ask about any disadvantages they have experienced being female in a male-dominated culture. Find men and women of color who are willing to tell you about their experiences dealing with prejudice. Then look for the similarities to and differences from your own experiences as a GBQ man. There is much to be learned by sharing pain and hurt; people can use this knowledge to heal, support, educate, and evolve as a universe of rich and diverse people.

About "Ethnic Homophobia"

Certain ethnic and racial groups often have their own forms of homophobia and prejudice due to strict gender and role expectations for men and women. If you are a GBQ man of color, your peers may feel that you've betrayed your male heritage. You may be thought unworthy, weak, or somehow less than a man because you are not interested in dating or marrying a woman. Men may also be condemned for having sex outside of a sanctioned marriage, for not carrying on the family name by having children, or for having nontraditional interests or characteristics. Prejudice in racial or ethnic groups may also originate from the misconception that being GBQ is about sex and promiscuity rather than love.

These issues need to be sorted through and understood. If cultural stereotyping and prejudice can be understood, then the ethnic GBQ man will better understand his community's discrimination against him.

Take the opportunity here to write about your "ethnic homophobia" experiences. If you are a white, Christian male of Western European heritage, you may want to use this opportunity to imagine how you would answer these questions if you were in different shoes.

Are you a man of color? Or are you from any group with strict codes for behavior based on gender or strict religious beliefs? If so, have you experienced additional prejudice or discrimination *within* your ethnic group because you are GBQ?

Describe your experiences.

As an evolving GBQ man, how can you positively change "ethnic homophobia" in your community?

Imagine a World without Judgment

Think about some of the freedoms that are denied to you as a GBQ man functioning within the heterosexual community. For example, certain things are "givens" for mainstream heterosexual partners, such as walking down the street holding hands or sharing a kiss in the shopping mall. Imagine how wonderful it would be if you could have these same freedoms as a GBQ man. Imagine being able to talk openly about your lover to the neighbor next door, dance with your man at the company function, hold hands comfortably in the movies, or mention your partner in a job interview or a casual conversation with a client.

Bob moved to San Francisco when he was thirty-four. He described his first trip to Castro Street, where he walked arm in arm with his boyfriend without self-consciousness or fear, as "truly exhilarating and freeing." Why shouldn't this be a basic freedom no matter where you are?

Imagine the basic freedoms you want as a GBQ person—what are they?

_____

_____

_____

_____

Isn't it time for the larger world to recognize gay and bisexual people as a viable part of society as a whole? Wouldn't it be better if those who are against GBQ folks could redirect all their energies to serious community and world issues such as creating peace, ending poverty, finding cures for diseases, helping kids stay in school, stopping abuse, and building communities instead of tearing them down and pulling people apart?

All GBQ men who participate as healthy role models by living openly and freely and working to stop discrimination are leading the way to a healthy future. What role will you play in securing this future?

14

From Here on Out

I am so tired of these stories about, "Oh the torture and torment of coming out." There's no torment in coming out. The torment is in being in.

—Armistead Maupin,
Tales of the City

You have made a choice to be more open about your sexuality, and in an extraordinary and wonderful way, there is no turning back. From here on out in your life, as your future becomes part of your history, you will reach out to the hands that welcome you, stand tall against the people who scorn you, and recognize the familiar faces of men like you. You will truly *see* yourself. You may have difficulty remembering details of your struggle to be true to your gay, bisexual, or questioning way.

This is your journey and no one else's. Whether you sleep exclusively with men, sometimes with women, remain hopefully perplexed, or walk both sides of the fence, your psychological, physical, and spiritual health is in your own hands. Whether you thrive or surrender depends on how you weather the winds of politics, hatred, and inner turmoil.

Being GBQ in Your Community: Assimilation versus Integration

How you fit into your overall community is a critical aspect of coming out every day. Start by looking at what it means for you to have a community that integrates you rather than assimilates you. What's the difference between assimilation and healthy integration? Good question.

- *Assimilation* is comparable to absorption. It means that you change or give up parts of yourself in order to blend in and live up to the dominant culture's expectations of you. When a GBQ man is assimilated, he is altered; he may change the way he loves, dresses, talks, and expresses himself.

- *Integration* is comparable to uniting and desegregating. It means you continue to express your true self as you coexist with other members of society.

Perhaps the most desirable alternative for you as a GBQ man is to maintain your own unique characteristics by choosing your own subculture and be integrated into the surrounding culture, without necessarily accepting all of its values, language, religion, mores, and norms.

Why We Choose a Subculture

Sometimes prejudice and discrimination push GBQ men away from the dominant culture into their own subcultures. Subcultures often exist alongside the dominant culture, sometimes with distinct values and behaviors and sometimes overlapping. The anger and hurt experienced because of judgment and rejection may compel GBQ men to mistrust and resent aspects of heterosexual society. For some GBQ men, the dominant culture's lack of diversity and imbalance of power demands a search to create separate GBQ communities that are special, sacred, and safe in their own right. Finding a subculture can help guide you on your path towards cultural integration while still maintaining your uniqueness.

Coming out is often a way for GBQ men to come to terms with their culture. Vance, for example, came out as a gay man at thirty, after years of trying to act and be straight. He dutifully attended mainstream social functions, listened to the "right" music, and dressed, walked, and talked in traditionally "masculine" ways. He felt these behaviors would bring him acceptance. They did not, however, bring him *self*-acceptance. He began to become disillusioned with trying to fit in and hide the emotionally expressive side of his personality. After Vance came out, he found he no longer needed approval from society in general. He dressed and behaved the way he wanted. He began to get his morning coffee from the café owned by a gay couple he'd met, because he felt comfortable to be himself there. He joined a gay and lesbian softball league and became active in the gay-positive educational movement. He became more accepting of people who were politically and culturally different from him, and incorporated some of his religious upbringing into his life. Vance successfully achieved the best of both worlds; he remained true to himself while still being able to live among the dominant culture.

How do you feel about the dominant culture versus a GBQ subculture? Do you agree that there is such a thing as a gay or bisexual subculture that is separate from the dominant heterosexual culture? Were you part of the dominant heterosexual culture before you came out as a GBQ man? Are you part of it now?

_____

_____

_____

_____

Integration: Is It Right for You?

Is integration a more "evolved" approach than assimilation? Some GBQ activists believe it is important to avoid assimilation so as to maintain your distinct GBQ identity. The thinking is that GBQ men must preserve their unique values, beliefs, behaviors, and interests rather than become "heterosexualized" (assimilated). Such assimilation may be evidenced by men marrying men in traditional ceremonies and garb, living in suburban homes doing suburban things, worshipping at traditional churches, and dressing and acting like other heterosexual men. These GBQ guys are sometimes characterized as "lost" or negatively acculturated into heterosexual society, just as African, Asian, Latino, and ethnically diverse Americans are sometimes condemned for abandoning their cultural heritage and taking on the dominant "American" way (working in corporate jobs; dressing, talking, and acting "white").

This opinion, too, is a type of prejudice. In truth, free choice means each person—gay, bisexual, straight, whatever—must decide alone how he or she wants to interrelate with the dominant culture. Indeed, the best definition of the "American" way should be an integrated society, where each person is a separate but equal part of the whole.

If you are GBQ and were raised as a heterosexual male in Western society, you no doubt have felt a culture clash. It's likely, however, that as a child you adopted the dominant cultural ways while knowing you were different because of your sexual orientation. As a GBQ adult, you may have eschewed the dominant culture and, in the process of coming out, assimilated into the "gay or bisexual" culture. It may be that you are now ready for integration into your general community as another step in your coming-out journey.

Lane, a bisexual man, was integrated into his heterosexual community in terms of his middle-class work ethics and living environments. He continued to believe in the values and traditions of his parents and their religion. Yet he also belonged to a bisexual subculture, in which he valued the importance of human rights and dignity for racial diversity and GBQ people. He found his own way, choosing to integrate into the dominant society by being open about his sexuality with friends and colleagues, participating in local gay and bisexual community organizations, and speaking up for the underdog in his work as a social worker at a health center.

Think about the meanings of assimilation and integration. How have you as a GBQ man been assimilated or integrated (or both) into your dominant culture? Consider what has happened to your values, norms, beliefs, actions, traditions, and practices over the course of your life in the dominant culture.

_____

_____

_____

_____

In terms of assimilation and integration, what do you think is right for you as a GBQ man? Is it important for you to define yourself as separate from the dominant heterosexual culture? If you aren't already doing this, how would you like to express your unique GBQ cultural identity? What teachings, rituals, and behaviors do you want to maintain from the culture in which you were raised? From the culture you live in now?

_____

_____

_____

_____

Visualizing Integration and Beyond

Visualize the kind of culture and society *you* want to live in. In creating your vision, keep the following questions in mind:

- How do people get along with one another?

- How are GBQ people treated? Transgendered people? People of color? Physically or mentally challenged people?

- How are people who don't belong to the dominant culture treated? Are they integrated into society? What would a multi-cultural society look like for you? How is diversity celebrated?

- How are subcultures, like GBQ, Jewish, Latino, and so on, integrated into society?

- How is discrimination and prejudice dealt with?

Now think about how it would feel to live, work, and play in your ideal environment. How would you express and celebrate your passions, values, and spirituality in such a society?

Write down your vision.

_____

_____

_____

_____

_____

_____

_____

_____

_____

Believe That You Can Make It Happen

Do you believe in your vision? Is it attainable? Maybe the culture you have imagined seems too idealistic, unrealistic, or unattainable to you at this point. But keep in mind the power of knowing what you want and making it a goal—even a goal this big isn't impossible.

When you dream of a large-scale community, when you visualize your global cultural goal of how *you* want to live, believe that your contributions can make a difference. Recall the discussion in chapters 10 and 11 about the importance of knowing what you want in friendships, love partners, and community. This is just as important on a large scale—even if you aren't politically active, your small decisions can make a difference. For example, a gay friend of mine told me a wonderful story about his in-laws' fiftieth wedding anniversary: When the music began to play, he and his lover of many years got up and danced until the wee hours of the morning, with the love and support of all the extended family. A small, but significant waltz in the right direction for all gaykind. I think of these actions as models of courage that pave the way for change. Eventually, they will have an effect on the public psyche by challenging stigmatization and encouraging integration for you and every GBQ person out there.

What can you do now to add to this effect? Use your vision to open your eyes. By imagining what you want from your culture, you can begin to see what may already be in front of you. Acknowledge the smile on the old man's face in the crowd, the generosity of your next-door neighbor. Random acts of kindness are happening all around you—think of the guy who helped you get your pitiful car to the gas station after you'd been stuck for hours on some lonely highway. Open your ears and eyes to the stories about the community working to rebuild the synagogue burned by bigots, or the company granting domestic partners benefits and promoting women and people of color to positions of real leadership. Pay attention to your own strengths, and acknowledge and build on them to create what you want in your world—even if it is small in comparison to the overwhelming prejudice and lack of integration that you see around you. Is the glass half full or is it half empty? It's up to you.

Cherish your vision of GBQ inclusiveness. Do what you can to improve society's understanding of GBQ love and life. Develop relationships with uninformed people and help them to know the truth. Find ways to change existing discriminatory practices. Stand up and speak out with dignity. Protest. Write to the senator who backs that gay rights bill and perhaps write to the ones who don't.

Revise and update your vision as the meaning of diversity evolves for you. Remember how little you knew (even though you thought you knew a lot) as a young child or teen and notice how much more self-aware and enlightened you are now. Compare your past and present awareness, and commit yourself to building a culture of awareness and diversity that grows as you do.

GBQ People Making a Difference

Think about how far we have come in the past twenty or so years. No doubt there is a lot more work to be done to create a diverse, safe, and integrated culture for GBQ people in the United States and throughout the world. But at least we're on our way.

There are many examples of how GBQ folks have managed to integrate into the dominant culture. Can you think of some? It was only a few years ago that Elton John was rumored to be bisexual but wouldn't talk about it; his public image is much different today. Not so long ago, television programs and movies rarely, if ever, had a gay character unless he or she was negatively stereotyped. But today we can watch gay and lesbian entertainers and events by the dozens. The political arena now includes openly gay legislators and committee members such as Gerry Studds, Barney Frank, Roberta Achtenberg, and Sheila Kuehl to name but a few. Margarethe Cammermeyer and Randy Shilts are almost household names.

Staying Out with Dignity:
The GBQ Man's Mission

Feeling proud of who you are as a GBQ man will instill self-confidence and help you find your place in the world. Pride and dignity are created from within and without and both are indicators of self-respect about who you are and what you do. When you value your personal strengths; when you choose not to go along with the status quo; when you learn from your errors; when you continually renew your sense of belonging through new and deeper friendships and partnerships; when you are active in your community and pursue activities that reinforce your GBQ identity—that is how you cultivate and express pride. That is your mission for coming out every day.

What inspires you to be proud of being a GBQ man?

_____

_____

_____

_____

Symbols of Pride

Here are several symbols that have come to represent gay and lesbian unity, freedom, spirit, and pride. All of this information can be found in *The Gay Almanac* (1996).

Freedom Rings

Created in 1991 by New York designer David Spada, this symbol is made up of aluminum rings that are different colors of the rainbow and are worn on a chain. The rings together signify freedom, pride, and unity.

Lambda (λ)

This symbol was first adopted by the Gay Activists Alliance in 1970 to symbolize the energy of the developing gay movement. The eleventh letter in the greek alphabet, lambda symbolizes kinetic energy in physics. It is now an international symbol of being gay.

Pink Triangle

During the Holocaust, Nazis arrested homosexual men and made them wear an inverted pink ("female-like") triangle as a form of identification. It is now a symbol of pride and remembrance of the persecution endured by homosexuals throughout history.

Rainbow Flag

Designed in 1978 by San Francisco artist Gilbert Baker, the flag's six stripes symbolize the diversity and unity of the gay and lesbian movement. It is composed of red for light, orange for healing, yellow for the sun, green for natural serenity, blue for art and harmony, and purple for spirit, perhaps relating to "Over the Rainbow," sung by gay icon Judy Garland.

Colors

- Lavender: It is a mixture of blue (male) with pink (female) and throughout Western history has indicated one's association with being gay.
- Pink: See pink triangle.
- Rainbow: See rainbow flag.

Continuing Your Journey

Being out with pride and dignity can manifest itself in many ways. It can be evident in everything you do. It can be there when you talk about your loves, passions, and interests; when you write a letter to the editor in support of a GBQ issue; when you put a rainbow flag on your car bumper; or when you have a ceremony to celebrate your love for your partner.

Dignity as a GBQ man grows and blossoms as a result of your efforts to share who you are, stand uniquely strong, integrate into your community, and contribute to the diversity of your culture.

What are some examples of how you have shown dignity as a GBQ man?

_____

_____

_____

_____

What do you want to do to strengthen your internal sense of GBQ dignity?

_____

_____

_____

What would you like to do to express your pride as a GBQ man?

_____

_____

_____

_____

Remember it is often the small things you do for yourself and others that will affirm your sense of pride as a GBQ man. Not everyone can make political speeches, ride on the pride float, or donate pro bono legal services. And you don't have to chain yourself to a redwood tree to show your commitment and pride; nor do you have to get arrested to make your point. Find your own way to express your pride as a GBQ man—be creative, unique, inspired, and above all, let your inner pride shine through as you come out every day.

Remember:

- This is *your* life: Come out to whom you want, when and how you want.

- Be safe and well: Know when it is and isn't safe to come out. Practice safe sex and care for your mind, body, and spirit.

- Stretch your comfort zones in order to grow as a GBQ man.

- Be a real person: Express your GBQ sensibility, sensuality, and love, in your unique style that reflects who you are.

- Build a healthy, whole self. Look for ways to thoughtfully and instinctively unite your physical, spiritual, and mental health.

- Be passionate and proud, face and overcome homophobia, and start to build your community.

Continuing your personal journey as a GBQ man means you weave the wisdom of your experiences to guide you to be your absolute best, giving ample time for rest and rejuvenation along the way. Continue to expand your support group of family, friends, and community. Regardless of whether you're nineteen or sixty-five years young, wealthy or poor, Irish or Australian, Catholic or Buddhist, married or desperately searching—your story is important to the growing anthology of wonderfully diverse and open GBQ men.

What do you think of your progress so far on your coming-out journey?

_____

_____

_____

_____

Go back to the first chapter and look at what you wrote about your reasons for reading this book. How have you progressed? How do your goals and GBQ issues then compare with where you are now? In your analysis, answer the following questions.

How has your coming-out process changed? And how has coming out changed you?

_____

_____

_____

_____

How have your views of yourself and your circumstances changed?

_____

_____

_____

_____

Are you more confident and comfortable with being out? In what ways?

_____

_____

_____

_____

How have your views of others in your life, including your family members, people who disapprove of your sexuality, and homophobic people, changed?

_____

_____

_____

_____

What's left for you to accomplish in your coming-out journey?

_____

_____

_____

_____

Think about what you want to accomplish in the next one to five years as an out GBQ man in order to maximize your well-being (and have some fun) in terms of

•   Identity

_____

_____

- Intimacy

_____

_____

- Relationships

_____

_____

- Spirituality

_____

_____

- Physical health

_____

_____

- Sex

_____

_____

- Creativity

_____

_____

- Fun

_____

_____

- Other

_____

_____

Some General
Coming-Out Guidelines

You've now explored the ins and outs of being out as a GBQ man. In summary and as a general framework to your coming-out process, keep the following guidelines in mind. Remember that coming out as a GBQ man

- Is a *process*; it is a day-to-day journey
- Is always *your* decision to do or not do

- May be a more complex decision if you're HIV-positive; coming out about your sexuality and sharing your HIV status are separate issues, but they may be connected in terms of your own level of comfort

- Is a unique event that's individual to you; it depends on your personality, age, developmental life cycle, community, society, geographic area, culture, race, and so on

- May reveal surprises about your relationships: some friendships may not survive, others will flourish; some areas of support may dissolve and some may become enriched and even better

- Will, eventually, make you stronger—emotionally and spiritually

- Is for the rest of your life

Good luck on your journey. Onward and outward!

Workshops and Lectures

Bret Johnson offers trainings for professional, public lectures, and workshops for gays, lesbians, bisexuals, and questioning people. If you are interested in bringing one to your area he may be contacted at the address below.

Dr. Johnson welcomes your feedback, responses, and ideas regarding the material and exercises in this book. He regrets that he is unable to answer individual letters, phone calls, or requests for referrals. If you write regarding this book, please indicate whether quotes from your letter can be used in trainings or future books.

Bret Johnson, Ph.D.
P. O. Box 231
Saratoga, CA 95871-0231

Resources

This list is in no way comprehensive: inclusion does not suggest endorsement (although most are favorites or have proven reliable to GBQ men); nor does exclusion of a resource suggest a lack of usefulness or quality. This brief list provides a sampling of resources that are handy and are used frequently. A state-by-state listing of resources was not possible, but some tried-and-true national resources are included. Please be aware that addresses, numbers, and the resources themselves are constantly changing due to moves, changes in funding and such. To facilitate finding what you need, the books, agencies, organizations, groups, and so on, have been listed under general topic areas.

For a more complete listing of resources that are up to date, check some of the general reference categories on the Internet. Also check out *The Gay Almanac*, which I have used extensively in compiling my list—it's filled with fascinating trivia on GBQ men; it's a must for every GBQ man's library.

Abuse
Agencies/Organizations

Parents United and Adults Molested as Children, 615 15th Street, Modesto, CA 95354, 209-572-3446.
Provides support and counseling.

SCAP (Survivors of Childhood Abuse Program), 15757 N. 78th, Scottsdale, AZ 85260, 800-790-2445 or phone the National Childhood Abuse Hotline at 800-422-4453
Education, training, consultation, advocacy, networking, and resources for adults abused as children.

Books

Davis, L. 1990. *The Courage to Heal Workbook: For Women and Men Survivors of Child Sexual Abuse.* New York: Harper & Row.

Gil, E. 1983. *Outgrowing the Pain: A Book for and about Adults Abused as Children.* San Francisco: Launch Press.

Island, D., and P. Letellier. 1991. *Men Who Beat the Men That Love Them.* New York: Haworth Press.

Lew, M. 1990. *Victims No Longer: Men Recovering from Incest and Other Sexual Child Abuse.* New York: Harper & Row.

Adolescents/Youth

Agencies/Organizations

Bisexual, Gay and Lesbian Youth of New York (BiGLYNY) and Youth Enrichment Services (Y.E.S.). c/o The Center, 208 W. 13th Street, New York, NY 10011, 212-620-7310.
Peer-run social and general support network along with Y.E.S. Youth empowerment through creative arts and prevention services.

Hetrick Martin Institute for Lesbian and Gay Youth, 2 Astor Place, New York, NY 10003, 212-674-2400.
Education, advocacy, and social support for g/l/bi adolescents, homeless/runaways, and youths with HIV. Home to Harvey Milk High School, an alternative public school for g/l/bi youth.

Lavender Youth Recreation and Information Center (LYRIC), 127 Collingwood Street, San Francisco, CA 94114, 800-246-PRIDE

Books

Bass, E., and Kaufman, K. 1996. *Free Your Mind.* New York: Harper Perennial.

Pollack, R., and C. Schwartz. 1995. *The Journey Out: A Guide For and About Lesbian, Gay, and Bisexual Teens.* New York: Penguin Books.

Videos

Homoteens. Joan Jubela. 1994. Frameline, 346 Ninth Street, San Francisco, CA 94103, 415-703-8650.
A portrait of five diverse New York City teens.

Out: Stories of Lesbian and Gay Youth. David Adkin. 1993. National Film Board of Canada, 1251 Avenue of the Americas, 16th Floor, New York, NY 10020, 212-596-1770.
A portrait of several g/l youth and families.

Coming Out
Books
For You

Corley, R. 1990. *The Final Closet: The Gay parents' Guide for Coming Out to Their Children.* New York: Editech Press.

Clark, D. 1990. *Loving Someone Gay.* Berkeley: CelestialArts.

Duberman, M. 1991. *Cures: A Gay Man's Odyssey.* New York: Dutton.

Eichberg, R. 1991. *Coming Out: An Act of Love.* New York: Plume.

Isay, R. 1996. *Becoming Gay.* New York: Pantheon Books.

Kaufman, G., and L. Raphael. 1996. *Coming Out of Shame: Transforming Gay and Lesbian Lives.* New York: Doubleday.

Monette, P. 1992. *Becoming a Man: Half a Life Story.* San Francisco: HarperCollins.

Signorile, M. 1995. *Outing Yourself: How to Come Out as a Lesbian or Gay to Your Family, Friends, and Coworkers.* New York: Random House.

For Your Family

Bernstein, R. 1995. *Straight Parents, Gay Children: Keeping Families Together.* New York: Thunder's Mouth Press.

Fairchild, B., and N. Hayward. 1989. *Now That You Know: What Every Parent Should Know about Homosexuality.* San Diego: Harcourt Brace.

Griffin, C., M. Wirth, and A. Wirth. 1986. *Beyond Acceptance: Parents of Lesbians and Gays Talk About Their Experiences.* New York: St. Martin's Press.

For Children

Many books are now published for children of g/l/bi parents and relatives. You can access a list from PFLAG via e-mail: jeaneileen@ aol.com or Website: http://www.pflag.org.

Couples/Relationships
Agencies/Organizations

Partners Task Force for Gay and Lesbian Couples. Box 9685, Seattle, WA 98109-0685, 206-935-1206, e-mail: demian@eskimo.com.
A home page dedicated to the needs of same-sex couples. Active in civil rights for g/l couples. Booklet called Indispensable Guide for Gay and Lesbian Couples *available for a fee.*

Books

Berzon, Betty. 1990. *Permanent Partners: Building Gay and Lesbian Relationships.* New York: New American Library.

Driggs, John, and Stephen Finn. 1991. *Intimacy Between Men: How to Find and Keep Gay Love Relationships.* New York: Plume.

Isensee, Rik. 1990. *Love Between Men: Enhancing Intimacy and Keeping Your Relationship Alive.* New York: Prentice-Hall.

Marcus, Eric. 1992. *The Male Couple's Guide: Finding a Man, Making a Home, Building a Life.* New York: HarperPerennial.

Family (Your Own and of Origin)

Also see coming out section for books for your parents or other family members.

Agencies/Organizations

Children of Lesbians and Gays Everywhere (COLAGE). An offshoot of GLPCI (see below for details).
Organized by sons and daughters of gays and lesbians with chapters across the United States and beyond.

Federation of Parents and Friends of Lesbians and Gays (PFLAG), 1012 14th Street N.W., #700, Washington, DC 20005, 202-638-0243/4200, e-mail PFLAGNTL@aol.com.
Educates and supports parents and friends, and advocates for gays and lesbians.

Gay and Lesbian Parents Coalition International (GLPCI), P.O. Box 50360, Washington DC 20091, 202-583-8019, e-mail GLPCINat@ix.nexcom.com.
International advocacy, education, and support organization for gays and lesbians in child-nurturing roles. Offers Internet g/l news, coalition of U.S. support groups, newsletters, bibliographies, and sponsors national annual conference.

Books

Barret, R., and B. Robinson. 1990. *Gay Fathers.* Lexington, MA: Lexington Books.

Bozett, F., and M. Sussman. 1990. *Homosexuality and Family Relations.* Binghamton, NY: Harrington Park Press.

Martin, A. 1993. *Lesbian and Gay Parenting Handbook: Creating and Raising Our Families.* New York: HarperCollins.

Rizzo, C., et al., eds. 1995. *All the Way Home: Parenting and Children in the Lesbian and Gay Community—A Collection of Short Fiction.* Norwich, VT: New Victoria Publishers.

Magazines/Newsletters

In the Family: A Magazine for Lesbians, Gays, Bisexuals and Their Relations. Takoma Park, MD. 301-270-4771.

The Family Next Door (newsletter), Next Door Publishing, Ltd., P.O. Box 21580, Oakland, CA 94620, 510-482-5778.

Online

The Gaydada List. A listserver for gay men who are or want to be fathers. To subscribe, e-mail: majordomo@vector.casti.com.

The Kids of Gays List. For kids of all ages with gay, lesbian, bisexual or transgendered parents. To subscribe, e-mail majordomo@vector. casti.com.

Videos

Not All Parents Are Straight. Kevin Whiter. Available from Cinema Guild, Suite 802, 1697 Broadway, New York, NY 10019, 212-246-5522.
Profiles lesbian and gay parents in history in action with their children.

Straight From the Heart: Stories of Parents' Journeys to a New Understanding of Their Gay and Lesbian Children. Dee Mosbacher. 1994. Motivational Media, 8430 Santa Monica Boulevard., Los Angeles, CA 90069, 800-848-2707.
Academy award-winning documentary to help parents of g/l children. Addresses religious concerns.

Gay and Bisexual Interest and Reference

Agencies/Organizations

Senior Action in Gay Environment (SAGE), 208 W. 13th Street, New York, NY 10011, 212-741-2247.
Support groups, counseling drop-in center, women's events, HIV and seniors programs, homebound program, education, and community outreach.

Books

Aging

Duberman, M. 1996. *Midlife Queer: Autobiography of a Decade.* New York: Scribner.

Berger, R. 1995. *Gay and Gray: The Older Homosexual Man.* Binghamton, NY: Harrington Park Press.

Biography/Memoir (also see Coming Out section)

Louganis, G. 1995. *Breaking the Surface.* New York: Random House.

Morrisroe, P. 1995. *Mapplethorpe.* New York: Random House.

Vidal, G. 1995. *Palimpsest: A Memoir.* New York: Random House.

Biology

Burr, C. 1996. *A Separate Creation: The Search for the Biological Origins of Sexual Orientation.* New York: Hyperion.

Money, J. 1988. *Gay, Straight, and In-Between: The Sexology of Erotic Orientation.* New York: Oxford.

General

Abelove, H., M. A. Barale, and D. M. Halperin, eds. 1993. *The Lesbian and Gay Studies Reader.* New York: Routledge.

Bawer, B. A. 1993. *Place at the Table: The Gay Individual in American Society.* New York: Simon & Schuster.

Blumenfeld, W., and D. Raymond. 1993. *Looking at Gay and Lesbian Life.* Boston: Beacon.

Browning, F. 1994. *The Culture of Desire: Paradox and Perversity in Gay Lives Today.* New York: Vintage.

Garber, M. 1995. *Vice Versa: The Bisexuality of Everyday Life.* New York: Simon & Schuster.

Hutchins, L., and L. Kaahumanu. 1991. *Bi Any Other Name: Bisexual People Speak Out.* Boston: Alyson Publications.

History

Miller, N. 1995. *Out of the Past: Gay and Lesbian History from 1969 to the Present.* New York: Vintage.

Katz, Jonathan Ned. 1992. *Gay American History: Lesbians and Gay Men in the U.S.A.,* revised edition. New York: Meridian.

Spencer, C. 1996. *Homosexuality in History.* New York: Harcourt Brace.

Film/Video

Olson, J. 1996. *The Ultimate Guide to Lesbian and Gay Film and Video.* New York: Serpent Tail.

Reference

Dawson, J. 1996. *Gay and Lesbian Online*. Berkeley, CA: Peachpit Press, 800-283-9444.

National Museum and Archive of Lesbian and Gay History. 1996. *The Gay Almanac*. New York: Berkley.

Witt, L., et al., eds. 1995. *Out in All Directions: The Almanac of Gay and Lesbian America*. New York: Warner.

Spouses

Buxton, A. 1991 *The Other Side of the Closet: The Coming Out Crisis for Straight Spouses*. Santa Monica: IBS Press.

Hill, I., ed. 1987. *The Bisexual Spouse: Different Dimensions in Human Sexuality*. McLean, VA: Barlina Books.

Travel

Collins, A. 1996. *Fodor's Gay Guide to the USA*. New York: Fodor's Travel Publications Inc.

Kolber-Stuart, B., and D. Aiport. 1997. *Out and About Gay Travel Guides*. New York: Hyperion.

Workplace

Baker, D., S. Strub, and B. Henning. 1995. *Cracking the Corporate Closet*. New York: HarperCollins.

Minkens, E. 1995. *The 100 Best Companies for Gay Men and Lesbians*. New York: Pocket Books.

McNaught, B. 1995. *Gay Issues in the Workplace*. New York: St. Martin's Press.

Woods, J. 1993. *The Corporate Closet: The Professional Lives of Gay Men in America*. New York: The Free Press.

Bookstores

There are many wonderful small gay and lesbian bookstores throughout the United States and Canada. You can access an up-to-date list of gay/lesbian/bisexual bookstores via e-mail: leeph@netcom.com. Here are a few to get you started:

A Different Light Books, 489 Castro Street, San Francisco, CA, 415-431-0891; 8853 Santa Monica Boulevard., West Hollywood, CA, 310-854-6601; 151 W. 19th Street, New York, NY, 212-645-7573.

Crossroads Market, 610 W. Alabama, Houston, TX, 713-942-0147; 3930 Cedar Springs Road, Dallas, TX, 214-521-8919.

Lambda Rising Bookstores, 1625 Connecticut Avenue NW, Washington, DC, 202-462-6969 (also in Rehoboth Beach, DE), 1-800-621-6969, e-mail lambdarising@his.com.

Journals

Gay and Lesbian Quarterly. Contact: Christopher Alexander, ed. 981 Paseo Del Sur, Santa Fe, NM 87501, 505-983-7037.

Journal of Gay, Lesbian, and Bisexual Identity. 233 Spring Street, New York, NY 10013, Human Sciences Press.

Journal of Homosexuality. 10 Alice Street, Binghamton, NY 13904, Haworth Press.

Journal of Lesbian and Gay Studies. Newark, NJ: International Publishers Distributor, 1-800-545-8398.

Magazines/Newsletters

The Advocate, 6922 Hollywood Boulevard, 10th Floor, Los Angeles, CA 90028, 213-871-1225.

Anything That Moves: Beyond the Myth of Bisexuality, 2404 California Street #24, San Francisco, CA 94115, 415-564-2226.

Bisexuality (bimonthly newsletter), P.O. Box 20917, Long Beach, CA 90801, 310-597-2799

Genre Magazine, 8033 Sunset Boulevard #261, Los Angeles, CA 90046, 800-576-9933.

OUT, 110 Greene Street, Suite 800, New York, NY 10012, 212-334-9119.

Ten Percent, 54 Mint Street, Suite 200, San Francisco, CA 94103, 415-905-8590.

Online

General

America Online: Gay and Lesbian Community Forum: keyword GLCF; Planet Out: keyword PNO; InsideOUT: e-mail InsideOUT2@aol.com (youth magazine for g/l/bi).

Compuserve: PRIDE!

Out.com. (Daily gay news and reporting) website: http://www.out.com.

OutProud! homepage: http://www.outproud.org/outproud/.

Queer Resource Directory, "QRD" website: http://www.qrd.org/qrd/.

Massachusetts Institute for Gay, Lesbian and Bisexual Studies, 98 Wyman Street, Boston, MA 02130. 617-624-6730, e-mail: wymans19@nfi.com.

Spouses

Straight Spouse Support Network (SSSN), c/o Amity Pierce Buxton, 8215 Terrace Drive, El Cerrito, CA 94530-3058. 510-525-0200. e-mail KYUB40C@ prodigy.com or http://www.qrd.org/qrd/www/orgs/sssn/home.htm.

Bisexual Married Men of America (BMMA), e-mail: zacharya@umich.edu. *Unmoderated discussion group for bisexual and gay married men.*

Videos

Silent Pioneers. 1984. Lucy Winer. Filmmakers Library, 124 E. 40th Street, New York, NY 10016, 212-808-4980.

Health: General, HIV/AIDS, and Mental Health

Agencies/Organizations

Committee on Gay and Lesbian Concerns, American Psychological Association, 1200 17th Street NW, Washington, DC 20036, 202-336-5500. *Will provide help in finding a gay/lesbian affirmative psychologist in your area.*

Gay and Lesbian Medical Association (GLMA), 2773 Church Street, San Francisco, CA 94114, 415-255-4547. *Assists in finding a gay/lesbian physician in North America.*

National AIDS Hotline (CDC), 800-342-AIDS. *A twenty-four-hour number with HIV/AIDS information.*

Project Inform Hotline, 1-800-822-7422 (U.S.) or 1-800-334-7422 (CA) *Provides up-to-date information on everything you ever wanted to know about HIV and AIDS.*

San Francisco AIDS Foundation. 10 United Nations Plaza. San Francisco, CA 94102-4901, 415-487-3000. *Provides free information pamphlets on HIV and safer sex.*

Books

Mental Health

Alberti, R., and M. Emmons. 1970. *A Guide to Assertive Living: Your Perfect Right.* San Luis Obisbo, CA: Impact Publishers.

Alexander, C., ed. 1996. *Gay and Lesbian Mental Health: A Sourcebook for Professionals.* Binghamton, NY: Harrington Park Press.

Beattie, M. 1989. *Beyond Codependency.* New York: Harper/Hazelden.

Bourne, E. J. 1995. *The Anxiety and Phobia Workbook,* 2nd ed. Oakland, CA: New Harbinger.

D'Augelli, A., and C. Patterson, eds. 1995. *Lesbian, Gay, and Bisexual Identities Over the Lifespan: Psychological Perspectives.* New York: Oxford.

McKay, M., and P. Fanning. 1993. *Being a Man.* Oakland, CA: New Harbinger.

Hopke, R., K. Carrington, and S. Wirth. 1993. *Same-Sex Love and the Path to Wholeness: Perspectives on Gay and Lesbian Development.* Boston: Shambhala.

Laird, J., and R. J. Green. 1996. *Lesbian and Gays in Couples and Families: A Handbook for Therapists.* San Francisco: Jossey-Bass.

Matsakis, A. 1996. *I Can't Get Over It: A Handbook for Trauma Survivors,* 2nd ed. Oakland, CA: New Harbinger.

HIV/AIDS Treatment and Education

Bartlett, J. G., and A. Finkbeiner. 1996. *The Guide to Living with HIV Infection.* Baltimore: Johns Hopkins University.

Martelli, L., et al. 1993. *When Someone You Know Has Aids,* revised edition. New York: Crown Publishing.

McIlvenna, E., ed. 1992. *The Complete Guide to Safer Sex.* Ft. Lean, NJ: Barricade.

Odets, W. 1995. *In the Shadow of the Epidemic: Being HIV-Negative in the Age of Aids.* Durham: Duke University Press.

Magazines/Newsletters

AIDS Treatment News, 800-873-2812.
   One of the original newsletters, it offers informative, easy reading.
Art and Understanding, 800-841-8707.
   A visual/literary magazine about AIDS.
BETA (San Francisco AIDS Foundation), 415-863-2437.
   A magazine that offers Western and alternative therapies.
GMHC Treatment Issues (Gay Men's Health Crisis), 212-337-3695
   Includes some of the latest information on clinical trails.
POZ, 800-883-2163.
   An HIV/AIDS magazine with art, information about treatment, news, and personal interviews.

Legal
Agencies/Organizations

Gay and Lesbian Advocates and Defenders (GLAD), P.O. Box 218, Boston, MA 02112, 617-426-1350.

Lambda Legal Defense and Education Fund, National Headquarters, 666 Broadway, 12th Floor, New York, NY 10012, 212-995-8585.

LeGAL: Lesbian and Gay Legal Association, P.O. Box 1899, Grand Central Station, New York, NY 10163, 212-302-5100. Lawyer referral: 212-459-4873; pro bono committee: 212-459-4754.

National Lesbian and Gay Law Association, Box 77130, National Capitol Station, Washington, DC 20014, 202-389-0161.

Books

Curry, H., and C. Denis. 1988. *A Legal Guide for Lesbian and Gay Couples.* Berkeley, CA: Nolo Press.

Lambda Legal Defense and Education Fund, *The Little Black Book: This One Can Keep You Out of Trouble.* New York: LLDEF. (free pamphlet—contact 212-995-8585)

People of Color
Agencies/Organizations

Black Gay and Lesbian Leadership Forum, 1219 S. La Brea, Los Angeles, CA 90019, 213-964-7820.

National Latino/a Lesbian and Gay Organization (LLEGO), 703 G Street SE, Washington, DC 20003, 202-454-0092.

Trikone, P.O. Box 21354, San Jose, CA 95151-1354, 408-270-8776. e-mail trikone@rahul.net.

Magazines

Asians and Friends/New York, P.O. Box 6628, New York, NY 10163, 212-674-5064.
Monthly magazine for Asian and Pacific Islander gay men.

COLORLife!, 301 Cathedral Parkway, Suite 287, Annex Building, New York, NY 10026.
The lesbian, gay, two spirit, and bisexual people of color magazine.

Paz Y Liberacion, P.O. Box 66450, Houston, TX 77266.
Quarterly newsletter with g/l news about Latin America, Asia, Africa, and Middle East.

Politics/Activism/Antihomophobia
Agencies/Organizations

ACT-UP (AIDS coalition to unleash power), 135 W. 29th Street, 10th Floor, New York, NY 10001, 212-564-2437.

Gay and Lesbian Alliance Against Defamation (GLAAD), 8455 Beverly Boulevard #305, Los Angeles, CA 90048, 213-658-6775. New York:

212-807-1700.
National organization that advocates for accurate, nonhomophobic, inclusive portrayals of gays, lesbians, and bisexuals in multimedia forms.

Human Rights Campaign, 1104 14th Street, NW, Suite 200, Washington, DC 20005, 202-628-4160.
Nation's largest gay/lesbian/bisexual civil rights group for health, safety, and rights. Lobbies for rights and supports congressional candidates for positive gay/lesbian/bisexual political actions.

National Gay and Lesbian Task Force (NGLTF), 1734 14th Street NW, Washington, DC 20009-4309, 202-332-6483.
National network of grassroots political and activist teams that advocates, educates, organizes, and lobbies for gay/lesbian civil rights. Also, Fight the Right project is organized to lobby for and provide information addressing misinformation and countering anti-gay religious/conservative right groups.

Queer Nation, c/o Lesbian and Gay Community Services Center, 208 W. 13th Street, New York, NY 10011, 212-260-6156.
Multicultural group aimed at direct action to fight homophobia, queer invisibility, and related oppression.

Books

Civil Rights

Fahy, U. 1996. *How to Make the World a Better Place for Gays and Lesbians.* New York: Warner.

Vaid, U. 1996. *Virtual Equality.* New York: Doubleday.

Homophobia

Berzon, B. 1995. *Setting Them Straight: You Can Do Something About Bigotry and Homophobia in Your Life.* New York: Plume.

Blumenfeld, W., ed. 1992. *Homophobia: How We All Pay the Price.* Boston: Beacon Press.

Herek, G., and K. Berrill, eds. 1992. *Hate Crimes: Confronting Violence Against Lesbians and Gay Men.* Newbury Park, CA: Sage Publications.

Spirituality
Agencies/Organizations

There are g/l/bi organizations for almost every religious group and denominations—this is a sampling.

Dignity/USA (Roman Catholic), 1500 Massachusetts Avenue NW, Suite 11, Washington, D.C. 20005, 202-861-0017 or 800-877-8797.

Radical Faeries, Pagan/Nature/Gay Spiritual Movement—ask around, check your local papers for group gatherings and functions—P.O. Box 1251, Canal Street Station, New York, NY 10013.

San Francisco Zen Center, 300 Page Street, San Francisco, CA 94102, 415-863-3136.

Unitarian Universalist Office for Lesbian, Bisexual, and Gay Concerns, 25 Beacon Street, Boston, MA 02108, 617-742-2100 ext. 470.

World Congress of Gay and Lesbian Jewish Organizations, P.O. Box 3345, New York, NY 10008-3345, 201-798-6383.

Books

Boswell, J. 1994. *Same-Sex Unions in Pre-Modern Europe.* New York: Villard.

Boswell, J. 1980. *Christianity, Social Tolerance, and Homosexuality.* Chicago: University of Chicago Press.

Boyd, M., and N. Wilson, eds. 1991. *Amazing Grace, Stories of Lesbian and Gay Faith.* Freedom, CA: Crossing Press.

Conner, R. 1993. *Blossom of Bone: Reclaiming the Connections between Homoeroticism and the Sacred.* New York: HarperCollins.

Dean, A. 1994. *Proud to Be: Daily Meditations for Lesbians and Gay Men.* New York: Dutton.

Helminiak, D. 1994. *What the Bible Really Says About Homosexuality.* San Francisco: Alamo Square Press.

Neil, J. 1994. *The Church and the Homosexual.* New York: Farrar, Straus, and Giroux.

O'Neil, J. 1994. *Freedom, Glorious Freedom: The Spiritual Journey to the Fullness of Life for Gays, Lesbians, and Everybody Else.* Boston: Beacon.

Thompson, M. 1994. *Gay Soul: Finding the Heart of Gay Spirit and Nature with Sixteen Writers, Healers, Teachers, and Visionaries.* San Francisco: HarperSanFrancisco.

Videos

Always My Kid: A Family Guide to Understanding Homosexuality. Steve Baker and Russell Byrd. 1994. TriAngle Video Productions, 550 Wescott #400, Houston, TX 77007, 713-869-4477.
Challenges negative religious myths and stereotypes of g/l/bis.

1,500 Years of the Church Blessing Lesbian and Gay Relationships: It's Nothing New. John Boswell, Host.
Spiritually wise theologian and author John Boswell discusses Catholic history of same-sex marriages.

Substance Abuse
Agencies/Organizations

International Advisory Council for Homosexual Men and Women in AA, P.O. Box 90, Washington, DC 20044-0090.

National Clearinghouse for Alcohol and Drug Information (NCADI), P.O. Box 2345, Rockville, MD 20847-2345, 1-800-729-6686.
> *Via the U.S. Department of Health and Human Services NCDAI publishes a special lesbian, gay, and bisexual resource guide of studies and resource listings.*

Pride Institute, 14400 Martin Drive, Eden Prairie, MN 55344, 800-54-PRIDE.

Project Connect, Lesbian and Gay Community Services Center, 208 W. 13th Street, New York, NY 10011, 212-620-7310.
> *Model program for prevention, counseling, support, referrals, and education.*

Books

Kus, Robert, ed. 1995. *Addiction and Recovery in Gay and Lesbian Persons.* Binghamton, NY: Harrington Park Press.

Milton, A. 1995. *Men in Recovery.* New York: Perigee.

References

Bailey, J. M. 1995. Biological perspectives on sexual orientation. In *Lesbian, Gay, and Bisexual Identities Over the Lifespan: Psychological Perspectives,* edited by A. D'Augelli and C. J. Patterson. New York: Oxford University Press.

Berrill, K. T. 1992. Anti-gay violence and victimization in the United States: An overview. *Hate-Crimes: Confronting Violence Against Lesbians and Gay Men,* edited by G. M. Herek and K. T. Berrill. Newbury Park, CA: Sage.

Berzon, B. 1996. *Setting Them Straight: You Can Do Something about Bigotry and Homophobia in Your Life.* New York: Plume.

Bohan, J. 1996. *Psychology and Sexual Orientation: Coming to Terms.* New York: Routledge.

Boswell, J. 1994. *Same Sex Unions in Pre-Modern Europe.* New York: Villard.

Cain, R. 1991. Stigma management and gay indentity development. *Social Work,* 36:67–73.

Cass, V. 1984. Homosexual identity formation: Testing a theoretical model. *The Journal of Sex Research* 20:143–167.

———. 1979. Homosexual identity formation: A theoretical model. *Journal of Homosexuality* 4:219–235.

Clark, D. 1990 (revised and updated). *Loving Someone Gay.* Berkeley, CA: Celestial Arts.

Coleman, E. 1982. Developmental stages of the coming out process. In *Homosexuality and Psychotherapy,* edited by J. C. Gonsiorek. New York: Haworth.

D'Augelli, A., and C. J. Patterson, eds. 1995. *Lesbian, Gay, and Bisexual Identities Over the Lifespan: Psychological Perspectives.* New York: Oxford University Press.

Folkman, S., and R. Lazarus. 1984. *Stress, Appraisal, and Coping.* New York: Springer Publishing.

Fossum, M., and M. Mason. 1986. *Facing Shame: Families in Recovery.* New York: W. W. Norton.

Fox, R. 1995. Bisexual identities. In *Lesbian, Gay, and Bisexual Identities: Psychological Perspectives,* edited by A. D'Augelli and C. J. Patterson. New York: Oxford University Press.

Goldberger, L., and S. Breznitz, 1993. *Handbook of Stress: Theoretical and Clinical Aspects.* New York: Macmillan.

Gonsiorek, J. 1995. Gay male identities: Concepts and issues. In *Lesbian, Gay, and Bisexual Identities: Psychological Perspectives* edited by A. D'Augelli and C. J. Patterson. New York: Oxford University Press.

Grace, J. 1992. Affirming gay and lesbian adulthood. In *Lesbian and Lifestyles: A Guide for Counseling and Education,* edited by N. Woodman. New York: Irvington Publishers.

Herek, G. M., and K. Berrill, eds. 1992. *Hate Crimes: Confronting Violence Against Lesbians and Gay Men.* Newbury Park, CA: Sage Publications.

Herek, G. M., and E. K. Glunt, 1995. Identity and community among gay and bisexual men in the AIDS era: Preliminary findings from the Sacramento Men's Health Study. In *Psychological Perspectives on Lesbian and Gay Issues: Vol. 2. AIDS, Identity, and Community: The HIV Epidemic and Lesbians and Gay Men,* edited by B. Greene and G. M. Herek. Thousand Oaks, CA: Sage.

Hooker, E. 1956. A preliminary analysis of group behavior of homosexuals. *Journal of Psychology* 42:217–225.

Hopcke, R., K. L. Carrington, and S. Wirth. 1993. *Same Sex Love and the Path to Wholeness.* Boston: Shambhala.

Hunter, J. 1996. Gay and Lesbian Adolescent Sexual Identity Development. Presentation at the 18th National Lesbian and Gay Health Conference. Seattle, WA.

Isay, R. 1996. *Becoming Gay: The Journey to Self-Acceptance.* New York: Pantheon Books.

Jagger, M., and K. Richards. 1969. "You Can't Always Get What You Want." Abkco Records.

Kaufman, G., and L. Raphael. 1996. *Coming Out of Shame: Transforming Gay and Lesbian Lives.* New York: Doubleday.

Kinsey, A. C., W. B. Pomeroy, and C. E. Martin, 1948. *Sexual Behavior in the Human Male.* Philadelphia: W. B. Saunders.

Klein, F. 1980. Are you sure you're heterosexual? or homosexual? or even bisexual? *Forum Magazine,* Dec. 41–45.

Klein, F., B. Sepekoff, and T. J. Wolf, 1985. Sexual orientation: A multivariate dynamic process. *Journal of Homosexuality* 11(1–2):35–50.

Kubler-Ross, E. 1969. *On Death and Dying*. New York: MacMillan.

Landau-Stanton, J., and C. D. Clements. 1993. *AIDS Health and Mental Health: A Primary Sourcebook*. New York: Brunner/Mazel.

Leland, J. 1995. Bisexuality: Not gay. Not straight. A new sexual identity emerges. *Newsweek*, July 17.

Levinson, D. J. 1986. A conception of adult development. *American Psychologist* 41:3–13.

Masterson, J. 1988. *The Search for the Real Self: Unmasking the Personality of Our Times*. New York: The Free Press.

McKay, M., and P. Fanning. 1993. *Self-Esteem*, second edition. Oakland, CA: New Harbinger Publications.

Michael, R. T., J. H. Gagnon, E. O. Laumann, and G. Kolata. 1994. *Sex in America: A Definitive Survey*. Boston: Little, Brown.

Mills, R. 1995. *Realizing Mental Health: Toward a New Psychology of Resilency*. New York: Sulzburger and Graham Publishing.

Monette, P. 1992. *Becoming a Man: Half a Life Story*. San Francisco: Harper-Collins.

Money, J. 1988. *Gay, Straight, and In-Between: The Sexology of Erotic Orientation*. New York: Oxford University Press.

National Museum and Archive of Lesbian and Gay History. 1996. *The Gay Almanac*. New York: Berkley Books.

Pillard, R. C., and J. D. Weinrich, 1986. Evidence of familial nature of male homosexuality. *Archives of General Psychiatry* 43:808–812.

Potter-Efron, R., and P. Potter-Effron. 1989. *Letting Go of Shame*. New York: HarperCollins.

Rust, P. C. 1993. "Coming out" in the age of social constructionism: Sexual identity formation among lesbian and bisexual women. *Gender and Society* 7(1):50–77.

———. 1992. The politics of sexual identity: Sexual attraction and behavior among lesbian and bisexual women. *Social Problems* 39(4):366–386.

Savin-Williams, R. C., and K. M. Cohen. 1996. *The Lives of Lesbians, Gays, and Bisexuals*. Orlando, FL: Harcourt Brace and Co.

Seigel, S., and E. Lowe. 1994. *Uncharted Lives: Understanding the Life Passages of Gay Men*. New York: Dutton.

Thompson, M. 1994. *Gay Soul: Finding the Heart of Gay Spirit and Nature*. San Francisco: HarperSanFrancisco.

Twining, A. 1983. Bisexual women: Identity in adult development. Doctoral Dissertation, Boston University School of Education. *Dissertations Abstracts International* 44(5):1340-A.

Weinburg, M., C. J. Williams, and D. W. Pryor. 1994. *Dual Attraction: Understanding Bisexuality*. New York: Oxford University Press.

Other New Harbinger Self-Help Titles